THE BOND'S
REVENGE

THE BOND'S
REVENGE

A GUIDE TO THRIVING
IN THE BOND MARKET

ALEX DOULIS

Stoddart

Published in Canada in 2001 by Stoddart Publishing Co. Limited
895 Don Mills Road, 400-2 Park Centre, Toronto, Canada M3C 1W3

Published in the United States in 2002 by
Stoddart Publishing Co. Limited
PMB 128, 4500 Witmer Estates, Niagara Falls, New York 14305-1386

www.stoddartpub.com

To order Stoddart books please contact General Distribution Services
In Canada Tel. (416) 213-1919   Fax (416) 213-1917
Email cservice@genpub.com
In the United States Toll-free tel.1-800-805-1083   Toll-free fax 1-800-481-6207
Email gdsinc@genpub.com

10 9 8 7 6 5 4 3 2 1

Canadian Cataloguing in Publication Data

Doulis, Alex
The bond's revenge: a guide to thriving in the bond market

ISBN 0-7737-6212-4

1. Bonds. 2. Bond market. I. Title.
HG4651.D68 2001   332.63'23   C2001-930635-0

U.S. Cataloging-in-Publication Data
(Library of Congress Standards)

Doulis, Alex.
The bond's revenge: a guide to thriving in the bond market / Alex Doulis. — 1st ed.
[128] p. : cm. Summary: A thorough review of all types of bonds, as well as the
secrets of hedging, offshore bond investing, and avoiding high management fees.
ISBN; 0-7737-6212-4 (pbk.)
1. Bonds. 2. Investing. 3. Municipal bonds. I. Title.
332.6323 21 2001 CIP

Cover design: Angel Guerra
Cover illustration: Craig Livesey / five:seventeen
Text design: Tannice Goddard

The Canada Council | Le Conseil des Arts
FOR THE ARTS | du Canada
SINCE 1957 | DEPUIS 1957

*We acknowledge for their financial support of our
publishing program the Canada Council, the Ontario Arts
Council, and the Government of Canada through the
Book Publishing Industry Development Program (BPIDP).*

Printed and bound in Canada

To my son, Christos,
my first bonding experience.

Contents

Introduction: Escaping from the Casino Royale

You will buy bonds. Either in a fund or in your own hands. This will happen when you get older. Don't even think of doing otherwise. Instead, settle down and read this book.

In case you don't believe me, let me outline the alternative course of events. Let's suppose you are now 60 years old and you are drawing on your RRSP, RRIF, IRA, or 401k that is fully invested in mutual funds. How do you get the $40,000 you need to survive this year? Wait for a payout? Not likely, since you need the money now. You could sell some of your funds, but which ones? Certainly not the one outperforming the others, as your total portfolio performance would go down. Perhaps the laggard? That one might outperform if the market moves from bullish to bearish or vice versa. Or, suppose the market is just roaring ahead and the fund is increasing daily. How could you possibly sell and give up part of those great future gains? Worse yet, imagine that the market is in the dumps and you have to sell: you are going to take some losses and miss out on the market turnaround. In other words, you can't sell each year and not have some misgivings.

If the stock market goes into a prolonged slump — and remember that the Japanese market, which represents the world's second-largest economy, hasn't seen its highs of 1990 — how are you going to live?

To overcome these problems, the vast majority of retirees are escaping from the Casino Royale of the stock market. They have moved from equity to debt investments upon retirement. The smarter ones started moving their portfolios into increasing amounts of debt securities after they passed the 50-year-old mark. You might fear outliving your money, but worse still is the thought of the market taking away your money before you even have a chance to outlive it.

I know you are skeptical about moving into the bond market, because you bought this book. For years, you have listened to the vendors of mutual funds tell you how the equity market has far outperformed the debt market. I am sure you understand that the purveyors of equity mutual funds will cast the fixed-income market in the worst light. Sure, they sell bond funds, but by the nature of the beast, both the commissions and the management fees are lower than for equity funds. Vehicle vendors would have you believe that if you buy a Rolls-Royce, you will get down the highway at rush hour faster than if you drive a Honda Civic. It would be foolish to believe this were true just because you paid more for the car. But this is pretty well the sales pitch for mutual funds. On an open road, and under the right circumstances, the Rolls *will* get you there faster. But the road to investment returns, like the highway, is not necessarily smooth.

You've put a lot of effort into understanding, and possibly paid a lot to learn about, investments. If you are like most of us, you invested on your own at first. After one of the many debacles and market slumps, you realized that you did not have the ability to be an investment professional as well as a full-time earner in some other field.

The obvious solution was to use professional investment management. No more hot tips, rumours, or sweet new issues. The mutual-fund manager would take care of all that, and you would only need to know which mutual fund to buy to live happily ever after.

It was at this point that you discovered that not all funds are created equal; they are differentiated on the basis of country, industry, risk, management costs, and objectives. Then there are the fund managers. The great ones provide capital gains superior to the market averages. But who are the great ones and will they always be great?

You had to learn about fees. Were they front end, back end, or no load? What about management expenses? Were all of your gains being consumed by the management fees? Eventually, you mastered the ins and outs of fees as well.

Now the bad news: you've got more to learn. Specifically, if you are over 45 years old, it is time to learn about the bond market. For years, you've been shown the graphs of how equity earnings always outperform interest earnings. But people seldom ask which interest earnings or which equity earnings are featured. Better yet, if it is so easy to win in the stock market, why aren't we all rich? Why do the stockbrokers and fund managers have yachts while their clients don't?

Let us examine the claims made about equity funds versus fixed-income investments. Imagine you work for the marketing department of a mutual-funds company and want to show that mutual funds are better than bond funds. First, you choose an equity index as your benchmark. What's the best choice? If you want to show equity in the best light, choose New York's Dow Jones Industrial Average. This barometer of stocks has been around since 1896, so you've ostensibly got over 100 years of market history to which you can refer. But the Dow Jones of 1901 is not the Dow Jones of 2001. In fact, there is only one company of the original twelve still in the index: General Electric. What happened to the dropouts? The Dow Jones drops any company from its index that is no longer representative of the U.S. economy. In other words, companies like National Leather fell by the wayside when leather was replaced by other materials and the company slid into decline. So the index is always updated to include the new, rising stars. IBM is in the index, and it didn't exist before 1900. The index is always being updated to take out the laggards and put in the rising stars. Therefore, the index will always be rising.

Now, if you want to make the fixed income market look bad, use the GIC, or Guaranteed Investment Certificate, as your comparison. GICs have a low interest rate because of the low risk attached to the investment. A GIC is essentially an IOU issued by a bank for a period of a year or less. The issuer is a rock-solid institution, and the period during which your money is at risk is very short.

Look at the yield curves shown on the next page. (A yield curve is the interest rate that prevails for similar instruments as the period of maturity changes.) If you lend money for a long time, you want a higher interest payment than you would for an overnight loan because of the uncertainty of the economic and political conditions that will prevail during the life of the loan.

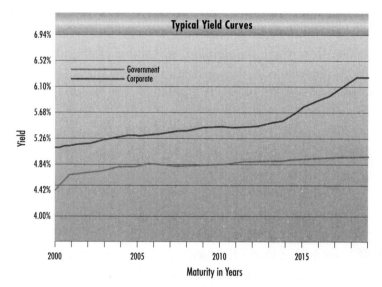

Let's say that you realize it wouldn't be fair to use the GIC as a benchmark. To avoid being racked by guilt, you choose, instead, to compare the best-growing index with a slightly more representative investment, such as a government bond. Government bonds, though, are still considered the safest of all possible issues. The interest they pay is therefore the lowest of debt issues. As a rough general rule, the lower-tier corporate bonds have a yield almost 40 percent higher than top-grade governments of the same maturity.

So let's try to be intelligent, rather than just fair, in this comparison. Mutual stock funds are made up of shares in corporations. As I have mentioned, corporations issue other securities called bonds or debentures. A rational comparison would be between the two classes of corporate securities, and that is what you will soon see.

But let's first get down to basics. What is an investment? An investment is an undertaking that provides you with a return or payment in exchange for the use of your capital. Many people cannot separate that from a speculation, a term that derives from the Latin *speculari*, to spy out. A speculation is undertaken because the speculator believes he knows how future events will unfold. The person buying Bre-X shares at $28 believed that the next drill hole would add even more gold reserves to the property than had previously been discovered. The speculator buying Amazon.com at $120 believed that the inroads of e-commerce were infinite. The person who sold the Bre-X shares at $28 had to believe that there was no more gold to be found, while the short seller perceived a fraud. The person selling the Amazon shares at $120 could not accept the scenario laid out by the company's founder. Not one of those three people invested to get an ongoing return.

When you buy a corporate bond, you do so simply to get a return on your capital. The same goes for preferred shares. This is quite different from the speculator's act of buying a share or mutual fund with the intention of selling it at a gain in a month or two. An investor is a person who buys a fund or a company's shares and then holds the investment until either the fund no longer matches or outperforms a benchmark, or the company's outlook changes. So portfolio changes are seldom undertaken by real investors.

THE EQUITY MYTH

Invariably, when people talk about the equity or stock markets, they will quote you figures such as the Finnish market being up more than 60 percent last year, while the Belgian was up 40, and the American 14. But there will be no mention of the Brazilian market being off 40 percent or the Thai market having a similar dismal performance. Plus, the good news is always from last year, not necessarily next year.

The long-term picture is also quite different. Think about it. Can the equity markets continuously grow faster than the economy? In other words, does the industrial output of a country grow less or more than the valuation of that industrial complex?

Let's simplify the issue. If Zoom Corporation has the same earnings every year — say, $1 per share — would the price of Zoom's shares be worth more or less next year? Obviously, all other things being equal, the price of Zoom's shares next year will be the same as this year.

Let's take that a step further. Suppose we sold all the equity in the country to one large mutual fund and called it Zoom. If there is no increase in industrial activity next year, the value of all the shares in Zoom should stay the same, because the earnings will stay the same. However, if industrial activity increases, the earnings will increase and the shares will be worth more. The increase in the earnings of the shares in Zoom (the entire national economy) will be dependent on the increase in industrial activity. Therefore, the value of a national stock market cannot grow faster than the earnings of the economy.

In North America, over the last century, the growth in industrial production has been almost 4 percent annually. That has translated into a growth in the value of share markets of between 6 and 7 percent per year. These are the real returns after taking out the effects of inflation (10.09 percent average equity-market growth – 3.14 percent inflation). In other words, the value of share markets appears to be growing at a rate more than 50 percent higher than the general economy. How can that be?

The answer lies in the fact that the companies that produce the goods and services fuelling our economy are not financed by shareholders alone. There is, in addition to the money raised by share issues, the capital provided by loans from banks or investors. This capital does not participate in the earnings, but obtains a fixed rate of return.

If the corporation has raised half of the funds it needs from shareholders and the other half from lenders, and makes 10 percent on capital, who gets what? Well, the lenders provided funds at 8 percent, so they will receive only 8 percent on their 50 percent of the capital. The numbers look like this:

Loan capital		$50
Share capital		$50
Total capital		$100
Earnings of the enterprise	10% x $100 =	$10
Return to lenders	8% x $50 =	$4
Return to shareholders	$10 – $4 =	$6

What we see from this example is that while the lenders received 8 percent ($4/$50), the owners or shareholders made 12 percent ($6/$50). A good deal for the shareholders, no? Look, however, at how the shareholders' return was calculated. The shareholders received their return after the cost of the lenders' investment was paid. The lenders receive their return on investment of 8 percent, irrespective of what the company earns — even if the company loses money. It is because the shareholders risk receiving nothing, or even paying the lenders out of their own pockets, that they are given a better deal in good times. But look what happens when the return on capital slips to 6 percent:

Total capital	$100
Earnings of the enterprise	6% x $100 = $6
Return to lenders	8% x $50 = $4
Return to shareholders	$6 – $4 = $2

BASICS

What is a dollar worth? Today, it is worth $1. But would you pay $1 for a dollar that you would only receive one year from now? Of course not. You would figure out what amount of money you would need to invest today to have $1 in a year's time. At a 6-percent interest rate, an investment of $0.9434 today would provide you with $1 in a year's time.* The present value for a dollar to be delivered one year hence would therefore be $0.9434. What about two years or ten years from now? If interest rates were 6 percent today, what would you pay today to get $1 per year for the next ten years? From the table below, you can see that the answer is $8.36. That would be how much you would have to invest to receive $1 a year for the next ten years.

The Present Value of One Dollar in the Future		
Year	Value at 6%	Value at 10%
0	$1.00	$1.00
1	0.9434	0.9091
2	0.8900	0.8264
3	0.8396	0.7513
4	0.7921	0.6830
5	0.7473	0.6209
6	0.7050	0.5645
7	0.6651	0.5132

---

* The formula for this calculation is Present Value = Future Value x (1/1 + discount rate), where n equals the number of years in the future. In this example, Present Value = 1 x (1/1.06), or 0.9434.

The Present Value of One Dollar in the Future (cont.)		
Year	Value at 6%	Value at 10%
8	0.6274	0.4665
9	0.5919	0.4241
10	0.5584	0.3855
TOTALS	$8.36	$7.14

The table shows that the value of a dollar in the future decreases with an increase in either time or interest rate. This is an important concept in understanding the bond market, because a dollar gained or lost in the future is worth less to you today. The bond market is all about receiving money in the future.

If the start-up company that you are investing in promises that it will earn $1 per share five years hence, that would be worth only $0.75 at 6-percent interest rates, or $0.62 at 10-percent. The above table shows that if you were to buy a company share that would earn $1 per share every year for the next ten years, it should cost you $8.36 to buy that flow of cash if interest rates were 6 percent, or $7.14 at 10 percent. In market parlance, the share is trading at 8.4 times earnings with 6-percent interest rates, and 6.1 times at 10-percent rates. Another way of describing the share is that it has an earnings yield of 12 percent when rates are 6 percent, and 14 percent at a 10-percent rate. The price-earnings (PE) ratio is the reciprocal of the earnings yield. In other words, a 6.25-percent yielding bond has a price-earnings ratio of 1 divided by 6.25, or PE of 16.

The equity investor prices a common share based on what the market perceives the present value of all the future earnings is worth. The further away the earnings are, the less they are worth today. Also, the higher the interest rate, the lower the value of those earnings today, and hence the lower the share price. This sort of calculation and assessment is complex, because one can never be sure of what the future earnings of a company will be. This should also show why the stock market goes down when interest rates are raised. This is because the present value of those earnings has to be discounted at a higher rate, therefore lowering their value today. If this sounds confusing, simply compare the two columns in the table above.

A bond or debenture is a much simpler investment instrument, because there is much less uncertainty. The investors know in advance the return they will receive and for how long. In effect, the investors have rented out their money. Bond investors know that they will receive rent, or earnings, every six months. Share investors can only hope that they will receive their portion of the corporate earnings, either as a higher share price or dividend in the future.

WHAT IS A BOND?

The term *bond* is generic. As a result of sloppy usage, the word is often used to refer to a slightly different investment vehicle, the debenture. Both are essentially IOUs. In other words, each represents a loan made to a user of capital.

To start or expand any business requires capital. Let me give you an example. When I was a geologist, I used to examine mineral deposits to see if they warranted the exploration needed to develop them into mines. At one time, I examined a property in the coast range of British Columbia owned by a man named Ray Wheeler. The property had some merit, and I recommended to Ray that he option it for an equity interest to a mining company to finance some exploratory drilling.* Ray's response was that the company should lend him the money to do the drilling. This is how the conversation went, as I remember it.

"Well, sonny, you have your boss lend me the money, and I will arrange to have the drilling done."

"Mr. Wheeler, what will my employer have if the drilling is successful?"

"Sonny, your boss will get his money back and a pile of interest."

"And if the drilling is unsuccessful?"

"That's obvious. He won't have anything."

"I doubt my boss would lend you money to finance a drilling venture where the odds of success are 140 to 1. If you want him to take that kind of risk, you'll have to give him some ownership."

"I am not about to give away a piece of this wonderful property," he said.

"Then let's do it this way. I'll get my employer to lend you the money if you put up something in the way of collateral. Let's say, your house or vehicle."

"Are you crazy? You expect me to risk my house on a hole in the ground?"

There were a number of interesting concepts elucidated in that conversation. We were talking about an investment and risk was the issue. If you are going to put your capital into a venture with a high level of uncertainty, you want involvement as an owner, not a lender. You want a piece of the action as either a shareholder or partner.

---

* At this point, Mr. Wheeler owned 100 percent of the property. To entice the mining company to finance the drilling, he would have to give it a percentage interest in the property, thus diluting his ownership.

No one would simply lend Ray the money at this early stage with such huge risk. But let's visit the project some years later, after Ray's estate put his gold property first into a joint venture and then into a public company. Shares were sold and money raised to drill the property. The drilling outlined a million ounces of gold, which after extraction costs was going to net $150 per ounce, or $150 million in total. To process the gold required a milling plant costing $50 million. How can the money be raised for the plant?

There are three ways. One would be with further share issues, but that would have diluted to the interests of the current shareholders too much. The other two methods involve borrowing money. But why can the owners of the mining property now borrow money? Because they have an asset worth $150 million to pledge as collateral. If the current owners borrow the money needed for mill construction, perform poorly as mine managers, and fail to pay their interest, then the lenders will seize the collateral (one million ounces of gold) and then attempt to sell the asset to regain their investment. At the outset, there was only the speculation that there might be an asset lying underground. However, with no proof of the asset's existence, there could be nothing to pledge against a loan. Once you have an asset with discernable value, you can borrow.

The shareholders wouldn't necessarily have to secure a direct loan from a bank. They could also borrow the $50 million from a single lender. If the amount was too large for one person, then two or more people could provide the funds. In a situation like this, where there is more than one lender involved, a *syndicate* is formed to provide the needed capital. These people each provide a portion of the funds;

these portions are pooled and lent to the company. The syndicate will have the company's *bond* — now you see where the term originated — that the capital will be repaid. Let us say, for example, that the company knows of 30 people who could together provide that $50 million. The lenders would form a syndicate, pool their capital, and elect a manager of their syndicate. It would be inefficient to have each lender individually collect his or her interest and review the company's progress, so one person is entrusted with the responsibility of collecting the interest and disbursing it to the lenders in proportion to the level of their loan principal. Let's call this person the *trustee*.

The trustee will give the lenders each a piece of paper outlining the extent to which they have lent money, as well as the terms of interest and principal payments. We might as well call this a *certificate*. What kind of certificate? A bond certificate. The trustee will also have the borrower provide a legal document, called the *trust deed* or *indenture*, which outlines the obligations of the borrower to the trustee and, hence, the lenders.

What if one of the 30 lenders wants to cash in early and leave the syndicate because he has found another use for his money? The trust deed clearly states the time at which the loan is repayable, and that date is much later than our lender is willing to wait. This departing lender has the option of selling his portion of the indebtedness to another person, who effectively becomes a new lender.

What I have just described is how the bond market evolved. There was a market for loans, or, as we more commonly call them, bonds, well before there was a share market. The whole idea of share markets evolved from the idea of bond syndicates.

In the example above, the borrowers had to pledge their

asset as collateral for the loan. What if a borrower has a going concern, with lots of assets and a steady stream of earnings? If such a borrower wanted a small amount of capital, we might be willing to lend it to him without demanding a pledge of capital, but instead just a commitment to pay. In this case, where there is a general obligation on the part of the borrower to pay, but no specific capital pledged, the paper representing the loan is called a *debenture* rather than a bond.

Now, what would it take to fund a nice little war, rather than a gold mine? Wars have always been costly undertakings, and there are few institutions that can supply the necessary capital. Wars are also highly risky ventures.

In the early history of man, capital meant weapons and soldiers. The smart guy who had a few soldiers at the ready would demand a piece of the deal. In other words, he wasn't willing to risk his capital (weapons and soldiers) on a loan basis. Instead, he would ask for his cut: "If we beat the other guys for you, not only do I want the rape-and-pillage option, but also part of the opponents' nice land holdings and the ability to tax."

As nations arose, it became a little difficult to give out so much of the pie to the average warlord. At this point, the belligerents turned to the banks. It was difficult for a bank to say no to Napoleon. Also, remember that this was a high-risk venture. If you lent to the loser, you would be out of pocket. Alas, hedging was born. When Napoleon faced Wellington at Waterloo, the Rothschild banking family lent to both sides. The interest rates were so high that it didn't matter who won. What they lost with Napoleon was more than made up for by what they made on Wellington.

It was, in fact, wartime borrowing that gave rise to the welfare state and the government borrowing necessary to finance it. When governments discovered that there was a source of funding for war, they began to ask if the same arrangement couldn't also apply to peace. Governments discovered that they could easily buy today's votes with loans coming due in the distant tomorrow. At first, governments borrowed for projects, such as dams, bridges, and roads. These required funding and gave rise to government bonds. "Turnpikes," or toll roads, for instance, were built with borrowed money. The tolls eventually paid back the loan. The public works were the asset pledged against the loan. But then governments realized that this was such a large pool of money that they could even tap into it without having to make a specific pledge. The lenders knew that the government had the right to tax, and therefore had the ability to pay. The government bond was considered riskless. But wait! Remember those lovely engravings, Czarist Russian bonds? Aren't they used to paper walls, as are the Chinese government's pre-1949 bonds?

The truth is that the government bond is not the safe haven many think it is. That faith is dependent on the belief that a new government won't repudiate the bonds and refuse to pay. In recent years, even existing governments have reneged on their loans. They have cited their inability to pay and rescheduled their debts. These governments were unable to pay because they used the money to bribe politicians, their hangers-on, or the voters. No asset was built with the borrowed funds and, hence, no cash flow was generated to repay the loan or its interest. In many ways, the corporate market is safer than the government one, because if the borrower defaults the lender can at least seize the corporation's assets.

Having said all that, let my old friend Stewart tell you his story.

1

We Go on a Vacation

Martha had decided that, this spring break, we would vacation in Viareggio. I was perplexed. I got out the atlas and found Viareggio on the west coast of Italy, near the northern end of the country. A bizarre choice, to say the least. The whole idea of going to Europe during our kids' spring break was that we would avoid the tourists and get cheap rates. But first I would have to sell the idea to our offspring. I decided to use the term Riviera. Things went downhill from there.

"Duncan, your mother and I have arranged a wonderful spring break vacation in the Italian Riviera. I am sure you and your sister will be thrilled."

"Actually, Dad, I'm going to be studying for finals then. I want to get into Queen's University, in mining engineering."

"Well, that's a very noble thought, Duncan, but you've never studied for an exam for more than two hours in your entire life. What the hell are you talking about?"

"I'm sure you've read about the Generation X phenomenon. Nobody in recent university graduating classes can find a decent job."

"What are you talking about? I just read that some of the most trusted advisers to our country's leader are failed political candidates, failed provincial cabinet ministers, even failed stockbrokers. If they can find jobs, why can't intelligent university graduates?"

"Quite simply, Dad, they get their jobs by being the right kind of people."

He had a point. I had known one of these advisers, an airhead of magnificent proportions. But she had impeccable credentials: member of an ethnic minority, member of a big focused group of campaign contributors, holder of a Ph.D. in some academic subject or other. Regardless of the fact that she had never succeeded at any job she had undertaken, she was advising the leader of our country, apparently on how to accentuate the country's downward spiral.

Okay, I thought, one down, one to go. I felt sure that my lovely Katherine would not disappoint me. Her love for her father was almost palpable. I found her in the kitchen. The smells were overwhelming.

"What are you up to, sweetheart?"

"Daddy, this is a braised sirloin with a Marsala gravy. I am going to serve it with boiled potatoes and asparagus."

"Sounds great. You're going to make someone a great wife."

"Daddy, the majority of the great chefs in the world are men. Do they make great wives?"

From the look on her face, I knew immediately that I had screwed up again. I could never talk to this girl. Every time I said something to my daughter, it came out wrong. I was going to mention to her my desire for grandchildren again, but I decided to load that on Duncan, who might be more understanding.

"Sorry, sweetheart. What I meant is that you are adorable, talented, and intelligent, and you'll make someone a great companion through this thing we call life. But what I really want to talk to you about is the forthcoming spring break holiday. You'll be happy to know that your mother and I have chosen northwest Italy — the Riviera." This was only a minor lie, in that Martha had chosen the destination.

"Daddy. I would love to come, but I'm taking a remedial course in mathematics during the spring break."

"Okay, don't give me the song and dance about the Generation Xers. I've already had that from your brother. Why do you have to get your math marks up? Aren't you going into law or social work? Your save-the-world instincts should prevail there."

"I've moved on."

"Don't listen to that redneck brother of yours. Women are supposed to be more caring."

"There you go categorizing again. I'm going to try for mining engineering."

"That's your brother again. You won't like it. Boots, belt, headlamp. Are you nuts?"

"I believe in feminism. Whatever a man can do, so can I."

I was glad to get on that Alitalia flight for Milan. Bloody kids had lost sight of the objective in life, which is to survive. I made up my mind to find a great survivor while in Italy: my friend Angelo. The last I heard, he was in his native Italy.

2

I Get into a Scrape

Oddly enough, in talking to his ex-partners, I found out that Angelo was in, of all places, Viareggio. We had rented a smallish villa just on the outskirts of that city. We chose a small one because Martha had contracted to do a cooking course with Marcella Hazan in Bologna. This involved her staying in Bologna for a few days while I stayed in the environs of Viareggio.

It was a great place, with a beautiful, sandy beach and a plethora of good restaurants. What really struck me was the palm trees. The gardeners had somehow planted cacti at the top of the palms, just below the leaves, and these were in flower. As I wandered around, I could understand the charm of the place for Angelo: it had both good food and a vast number of ship chandlers.

While Martha was staying in Bologna, I looked around the boatyards of Viareggio to find my old friend. I knew this would not be a difficult task, since I either had to ask about the yacht *Amarone* or just sniff the air for the smell of Havana tobacco. I wasn't sure about the tobacco, as I had heard that Angelo's health problems had ended his cigar-smoking career. Finally, I found him in a yard to the south of the large shipbuilders.

Amarone was hauled out of the water and in a cradle in the yard. Angelo was listening to a tape of some opera, and dutifully scraping the bottom of the boat with a one-and-a-half-inch chisel.

"Hi, Ang. What are you up to?"

"I got your e-mail and was hoping you would stop by. Then I deduced that it was inevitable."

"What do you mean?"

"My wife is up at a cooking course in Bologna being given by Marcella Hazan. Need I say more?" Ang said.

"Gee, so is mine."

"Stewart, do you not see what is going on here? This is a conspiracy. Martha and Sarah have decided to take a cooking course in Bologna and dump you in Viareggio."

"They wouldn't."

"They did."

"Shit."

"Not to worry," Angelo said. "I've got another chisel and a box of Cohiba cigars."

"I thought you weren't allowed to smoke cigars anymore," I said.

"Partially true. I was diagnosed with a throat condition five years ago, and a doctor in England cut me off hard liquor and cigars. Two years ago, a doctor in Florida diagnosed me with colitis. He asked if I smoked, and with the zeal of the recently converted I raised myself to my full height and answered, 'Lips that touch nicotine will never touch mine.' The doctor replied that this was indeed a shame, as nicotine had been found to be a palliative for colitis. I assured him that the nicotine neck patches he was about to prescribe were unnecessary, as I had my own delivery system — one that involved Cuban tobacco leaves set into action by the application of a small flame. He said that if I did this once a week, I would be contributing to my longevity. The present point of contention between Sarah and me is what constitutes a week."

"That explains the cigar, but what's with the scraping?"

"Ah, yes, insurance. As you know, *Amarone* is a Hans Christian vessel, not a yacht. The company was too arrogant to call their sea-going boats yachts. It is built to last forever. Sort of. A few years ago, it was discovered that the plastic on the bottom of fiberglass boats was not impervious to water. Moisture did penetrate some of the outer layers of the gelcoat plastic by osmosis, delaminating the fiberglass. What I am doing is scraping off the bottom paint, after which I will lightly sand the bottom and cover it with epoxy, which is completely impervious to water."

"So you've got water penetrating the plastic," I said.

"Not so, old friend. But rather than take a chance, I am investing in some insurance. If I apply epoxy to the bottom, I can be sure I will never have a water-intrusion problem."

"Why not wait until you have a problem?" I asked.

"Stewart, by that time, I may be too old to wield a chisel. Boat maintenance is like life: you have to plan ahead."

"Ang, I had a helluva time finding this yard. Why didn't you move into one of the big yards closer to the harbour entrance?"

"The Mob."

"You were worried about the Mafia?" I asked.

"Yeah, the other yards weren't involved with the Mob, so I chose this one."

"Are you telling me the gangsters own this yard?"

"Yeah, they bought it ten years ago. At the time, there was a spate of break-ins of the stored boats. The gangsters found one of the possible thieves and broke one of his legs. They told him that if the yard was broken into again, irrespective of who was actually responsible for the damage, they would break his other leg. It is a system of enforcement used by the Israelis and copied by the Mob. As a result, there has never been a break-in here. The last place I left my boat was the island of Elba. Thieves broke into my boat and spent the night looking for weapons. They stole two pistols. When I reported it to the *carabinieri*, the first thing they did was ask me if I was insured! The second was to threaten me with the charge of improperly storing weapons, because the thieves had been successful, after eight hours of tearing my boat apart, in finding the cleverly hidden weapons. I replied that they could put their charge in one of their body orifices, seeing as they were too incompetent to ever find the evidence — namely, the guns."

"Isn't that a little aggressive?"

"Not really. When the boat was stored in Turkey, it was broken into and the same two pistols stolen. Within three weeks, the Turkish police had them back and the Romanian thief on his way to jail. The Italians are a much more developed society, therefore they never find their thieves. In Elba, the thieves broke into four boats in the yard where *Amarone* was stored, and managed to make off with my sixty-pound anchor. None of the stolen equipment has been recovered, nor will it ever be. You can therefore understand why I chose to have an incorruptible police force like the Mafia guarding my boat. There's nothing like private enterprise, you know. Hell, when I leave tonight, I won't even bother to put away my tools. But tell me, how is the offshore working for you?"

"Great. The inheritance from my Irish rogue uncle is in an offshore trust, similar to the one used by the Bronfmans, accumulating a future tax-free payout. I've also moved all our investment income offshore to protect us in our old age. You heard that the government is broke, didn't you? It can't pay the pensions and is cutting back on health care. So Sarah and I have become master criminals. We've bought some hospital insurance outside Canada, in case we get sick. It only costs us $3,000 a year for the family, and the worst the government can do is to fine us if we use it in Canada."

"What's this crap about the government being broke? Governments never go broke," Angelo retorted.

"Ang, have you heard about Brazil? Belly-up. I have it from a source in the Canadian government that the country's old-age pensions, which we all paid into over the years, will be means-tested starting in 2003 and over by 2007. Canada will become Brazil in 2029."

"Stewart, you always were an alarmist," Angelo said. "Ease up."

"Look, my source is an assistant deputy minister in National Defence. He heard it in a seminar given by the Department of Finance. If you're so confident, how come you fled the country in 1990?" I asked.

"Because I was being cautious. You are talking about panic.

I just wanted some safety from the goofs in the capital. I needed to ensure my survival. It's like putting epoxy on this old girl's bottom. It makes her impervious. While my savings were in Canada, they were not safe. Now they are impervious — no leakage to slaphead governments. When I left, all the investment funds and firms were talking about preparing for old age by saving money. A lot of good that does if the government takes away all your money after you've saved it.

"But look, the days are short now. I can't sit around and talk all day. Why don't you climb on board and get the extra coveralls out of the wet locker? I've got a spare chisel and lots of Moretti beer. We can do some real damage here."

I returned with my designer coveralls, opened a beer, and asked the question that really interested me: what about the bond market? People spoke about it in hushed tones, either because they didn't know how it worked or didn't want you to know. I was aware that Angelo had made a small fortune larger by investing in the bond market, but that ran against the grain of what I read in the popular press. It was common knowledge that the real road to riches lay in the equity markets. But here I was, working under the keel of a quarter-of-a-million-dollar boat, owned by a guy who had voluntarily *not* owned a share of equity for ten years. What was I missing? I may not be a genius, but I do know what I don't know.

"Ang, the beer is a great bribe, but I want more."

"More? You sound like Oliver Twist. That's Moretti beer, a fine old Italian owned by Labatt. What do you want, blood?"

"No, something even less tainted: information," I said.

"Well, if it's inside information you're wanting, I never traded in that and never will."

"In a way, it is inside information. I want inside information on the bond market. How it works. What it is worth. The real inside dope."

"You know, Stewart, you must be the tenth person to ask me that this year. What's going on? Are all you yuppies getting old?"

"What do you mean by that?" I asked.

"Well, the bond market is where most investors end up sooner or later, whether they know it or not. Even those who move their pension funds into annuities — whether it is an RRSP, an IRA, or a 401k — are actually investing in the bond market. And all the guys who blew their brains out picking stocks in the 1980s, then found that the mutual funds did no better for them than they did as stock-pickers, ended up in bonds. It is a rite of passage, like getting drunk for the first time."

"But I thought that the real investment money was made in the stock market," I said.

"Ah yes, Stew. You're just another victim of the equity myth."

3

I Almost "Myth" the Boat

"The equity myth? What the hell is that?" I asked.

"A rather twisted tale, the purveyors of which are growing in influence. The tale relates that equity markets vastly outperform fixed-income markets. The tale developed from the need of mutual-fund vendors to embellish the status of the products they are selling, and the desire of stockbrokers to earn commission from trading. You see, most equity funds have management fees double that of bond funds, and buyers of bonds are less likely to trade."

"But why do you call it a myth, Ang?"

"Stew, how well have the equity investors in Japan, the second-largest economy in the world, done over the past ten years? In real terms, they have lost 3 percent per year. What I am telling you is that the comparisons between equity and debt markets are seldom as they are reported.

"To begin with, the comparison made by the mutual-fund

vendors is usually between a stock-market index and Guaranteed Investment Certificates (GICs) or certificates of deposit. However, the stock-market index is not what you buy when you purchase a mutual fund. There are a lot of costs included in the mutual fund, which don't inhibit the performance of the bare index. Also, the instrument of comparison — the GIC — is the one with the lowest possible yield. It's sort of like comparing the tortoise to the hare, but using the slowest possible tortoise."

"I don't understand. I thought a bond is a bond is a bond, to paraphrase Gertrude Stein."

At this point, Angelo scrambled up the ladder and brought down a chart out of what appeared to be a newspaper.

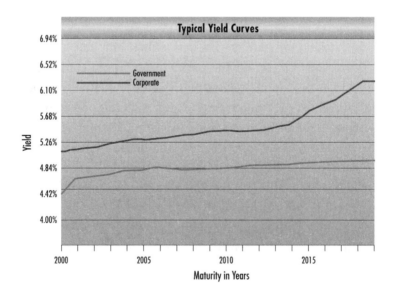

"Here, look at this graph. It illustrates what is called a yield curve. A yield curve shows you the return you can expect to receive for loaning money to someone for different periods of time. What do you see? The longer the term of the loan, the higher the rate of interest you can expect to receive. Why? Because more things can go wrong over a long period of time than during the short term. My risk in lending you 100 bucks for ten years is a lot higher than lending it to you overnight. Often, the mutual-fund ads compare their vehicles to very short-term securities, such as GICs, whose terms are seldom longer than a year or two. Bear in mind, too, that corporate debt starts off with a higher yield, which increases quite dramatically the further out in time you go. If you lend your money to one of the new technology companies, how do you know it'll still be around in 20 years' time? As such, once the term of a corporate loan goes beyond ten years, the interest rate climbs steeply.

"What investors seldom realize is that a share is similar to a bond, but has an infinite lifespan. The bond will mature someday at the price for which it was issued. What this means is that on redemption day, or possibly sooner, the investors are going to have their investment bought from them at a specified price per bond. A share will be in existence forever or until the company folds, whichever comes first. As an investor in shares, you may never have the opportunity to get your money back.

"The yield curve I have shown you is for government and top-grade corporate securities. These are supposedly the bluest of blue chips, but there are bonds that vastly outperform these issues. So the question arises: which bond market do you want to use as a benchmark to test the equity myth? Even better, which equity measure do you want to use as a standard? Which standard do you want for the stock market, Stewart?"

"God, that's a tough one," I said. "I could use Standard & Poor's 500, which is composed of 500 shares that trade on

U.S. exchanges. Wait a minute, let's use the Dow Jones Industrial Average."

"Why?"

"It's been around for more than 100 years and should give a pretty good portrait of how the market's performed," I said.

"Not a great choice, Stew. You see, only one of the original stocks that made up the 1896 index is still on the roster: General Electric. All the rest have been replaced a few times over, as the companies they represented declined or passed from existence. If a company has poor or no growth prospects in the foreseeable future, it is dropped from the index. As such, indices are not a great choice as a measure of equity investment performance over the long term. Instead, let's get down to basics."

"Ang, if you can't use stock-market indices as a growth measure, what are your choices?"

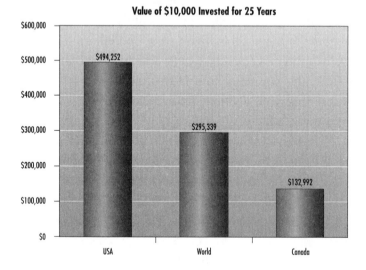

Value of $10,000 Invested for 25 Years

"Stew, I've got an even more daunting question: in which market do you want to invest? If you are thinking of Canada alone, you've got a rude surprise coming. Canada Trust conducted a study that showed if you invested $10,000 annually in the U.S., world, and Canadian stock markets over the 25 years ending December 1998, you would have the results shown in the following chart. As you can see, the growth rates are 16.9 percent, 14.5 percent, and 10.9 percent. That has to give you pause, because those are nominal returns, unadjusted for inflation."

"Is the time span of 25 years really representative?" I asked. "As we both know, the economy is cyclical. Maybe that 25 years is not representative."

"Boy, you are really tough, Stew. What will it take to make you believe? How about 67 years of experience?"

"Okay, I'll settle for 67 years," I said.

At this point, Angelo put down his chisel and climbed the ladder leaning on the side of the boat. I could hear things being moved around and, finally, a great bellow. "I found it!"

He showed me the following graph.

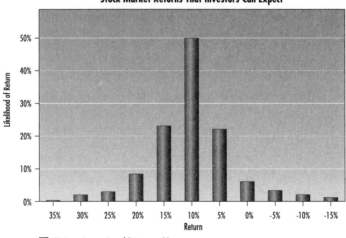

Stock Market Returns That Investors Can Expect

"What are you trying to show me with this?" I asked.

"First, you have to know what you are looking at. This is the result of a study done by Charles Jones and Jack Wilson, and published in the *Journal of Portfolio Management* in the fall of 1995. What the authors did was break the period from 1926 to 1993 into ten-year segments on a continuous rolling basis. You know, 1926 to 1935, 1927 to 1936, and so on, to finally end with 1984 to 1993. They then looked at what minimum average return an investor would have made in each ten-year period in the U.S. market. The interesting feature is that the span of time includes some of the greatest booms and slumps experienced by the market. What the results showed was that there was a minuscule chance of being in a ten-year period that would yield +35 percent or –15 percent. There was a 50-percent likelihood of earning 10 percent on your stock-market investment, a 27.7-percent chance that annual returns would be between 5 and 10 percent, and a 16.4-percent chance that returns would be 5 percent or less. The raging bulls would be surprised to hear that there was a 6-percent chance that annual returns would be negative over the ten years."

"That is staggering," I said. "Investors are looking at a crap shoot. Their most likely return is only 10 percent."

"That's a little extreme, but there is something you've overlooked."

"What's that?" I asked.

"Inflation. The academicians have looked into the question of equity growth over the years and have generally concluded that, in real terms, excluding inflation, U.S. equity markets have grown at roughly 7 percent compounded annually since the Great Depression."

"So what you're telling me, Ang, is that if I bought the market, or a representative basket of shares, I would make 7 percent compounded annually on my investment, and that would apply only if I bought the U.S. market. That doesn't seem like any great screaming hell," I said.

"You're right. However, inflation is the distorting factor. You see, we have never had a period in time when inflation was zero. Those same academicians who tell you that you will get $472,000 at the end of 30 years if you invest $5,000 for each of those years at that 7 percent, with no inflation, will also tell you that over that same long haul, the U.S. market will give you a return of about 10-percent nominal, or including inflation. So look what happens to your $5,000 per year at the nominal rate. You end up with $822,000. If you could buy a 10-percent-based annuity with that capital, you would receive $87,000 per year for 30 years. The hitch is that the inflation that worked for you while you accumulated your wealth would now work against you. You could retire at age 60 and expect to live for another 30 years, drawing $87,000 per year until your annuity ran out at age 90. But $87,000 might not be a lot of money by that time. Therein lies the rub, my friend: trying to get that guaranteed 10 percent per annum on a secure basis."

"Ang, you are confusing me. I thought you just said that I could expect 10-percent compound annual growth with my funds over the long haul in the stock market. Why can't I do that after I retire?"

"Stewart, the operative words there were 'secure basis.' Let me give you an example. Mrs. Iwata in Japan can count on the stock market giving her 10 percent over the next 30 years if she is 20 years old. But Mrs. Hayashi, who is 60 years old and has seen the market halve over the past ten years, hasn't necessarily got 30 years to regain her losses of the past ten years. It depends on where you are in the cycle, and nobody can guarantee where you will land up in the ups and downs of the equity markets. If you want that 10-percent nominal growth, I would suggest you start investing in your early 20s and keep it up until you retire. But if you are nearing retirement, then you have to carefully gauge in which ten-year period you might end up. Think about the graph of rolling ten-year periods I showed you."

"What about the bond markets?" I asked. "They haven't had any growth."

"Really? What about being paid 5.5-percent real return on your money every year?"

"A return of 5.5 percent? That's peanuts," I said.

"It's a question of yardsticks again," Ang retorted. "If someone is smart enough to have $100,000 in his hip pocket to lend to the bond market or to an individual, he is not so stupid as not to compensate for inflation. In fact, in their interest rate demands, lenders don't compensate for today's inflation, they compensate on the basis of expected inflation. If inflation today were 1 percent and I expected 6 percent over the life of the loan, I would tack on another 6 percent to the interest rate, giving a total of 11.5 percent. What can you get from North American government bonds today?"

"About 5.5 percent," I said.

"What are expected inflation rates in North America today?"

"About 1.5 percent," I replied.

"That means that you can expect to make a real 4 percent on your money in government bonds, and likely over 5 percent in corporates. If the expected inflation rate changes, the effective interest rate will as well."

"So, in the bond market, investors expect a real 4 percent from governments and 5.5 from reasonable grade corporates, right?" I asked.

"Yeah, and 6 percent or less in U.S. equity markets."

"What do you mean by the 'or less'?"

"Stewart, it depends on how you buy the market. If you do it through an index fund, you will underperform the index because of the management fees. You will do even worse if you buy an actively managed fund, because the fees are so much higher. In any given year, only 25 percent of the fund managers beat or match the index. There are few of them who do it on a consistent basis. Therefore, on the long haul, you will underperform the market unless you construct your own index fund and never trade. But then, what do you do when the components of the index change? You have to go into the market and incur costs. I went through these calculations with my son just a month ago. I've got the numbers in my chart table."

Angelo once more clambered up the ladder. I figured his total climb was about 12 feet. That meant he was lifting 200 pounds 12 feet every time he went up the ladder. No wonder he looked so good. He returned with a couple of envelopes on the backs of which were scrambled myriad numbers.

"Let's see," he said, "my boy figured the market would grow at a real 6 percent with a further 3 percent for inflation, giving a total of 9-percent annual growth. We took two funds out of the financial paper. One was an index fund with a management expense ratio of 0.31 percent and no load. It was the cheapest I could find. The second was a conventional managed fund with 2-percent load and a management expense ratio of 2.52 percent. Look at the results."

Ang showed me the envelope, which looked something like this:

Type of Fund	Initial Investment to Investor	Ten-Year Return	Rate of Return after Costs
Index	$100,000	$224,970	8.45%
Managed	$100,000	$154,578	4.45%

"Hell," Ang continued, "I can get you the index-fund yield in one bond: an Inco 7.75-percent convertible, currently selling at $910 to yield 8.84 percent. Regrettably, I can't think of a bond that will yield as little as the managed mutual fund."
At this Ang said, "Look what you've done to my boat. You've cleaned a whole swath. You work well for a novice. Just for that, I am going to buy you a great dinner."

"I can't go like this. I need a bath."

"Use the shower on the boat. I'm plugged into shore power, and the onboard water tank is heating as we speak. You first. I'm going to scrape around the through-hulls."

I climbed the ladder to the cockpit, thinking about what we had just discussed. The U.S. stock market on average has grown about 10 percent per year since the 1920s, if you include inflation, and 6 percent in real terms, or excluding inflation. On the other hand, the stock market in Japan has declined over the past ten years, and according to an article I read by Will Goetzman, a Yale University economist, the growth in thirty-eight other stock markets since the 1920s has been only 1.5 percent. Another author, Jeremy Siegel, an economist at the Wharton School of Business, calculated that from

THE BOND'S REVENGE — 37

1802 to 1992, the U.S. market had climbed 7 percent per year in real terms.

I grabbed one of Ang's envelopes and made my own notes.

STOCK-MARKET GROWTH RATES	
Market	Growth Rate
U.S. 1924 to 1964	6% compounded annually
U.S. 1802 to 1992	7% compounded annually
Other world markets, 1920s onward	1.5%

I was now really confused. I waited for Angelo to come up for his shower so we could talk about it. What I could see from the envelopes I clutched in my hand was that, with the fees involved in the actively managed mutual fund, I was going to vastly underperform the market.

4

Growth Pains

It wasn't until we were walking to the trattoria that I got a chance to ask Ang about the pile of numbers we had just been kicking around. What could I expect to earn in the stock market?

"Stewart, that's like asking, What is truth? There are a number of yardsticks, and as many yards. Let me ask you: Which market? What time period? How long? Real or nominal? In a fund? Active or passively managed? If you're talking about the U.S. market, it depends on when you invest. If you bought the U.S. market in the 1920s, you wouldn't have broken even until the late 1950s. If you had bought in the mid 1970s, you would have gotten your money back, in uninflated dollars, in mid 1994."

"Those are not impressive numbers. Why is it that I see all these ads pushing equity funds?" I asked.

"Look carefully at the pictures of those red-hot stock-jockeys. None of them was in long pants in 1974. The older ones have forgotten about the cobweb-covered phones on the brokers' desks in the late 1970s. The longest memory for most equity players is yesterday's closing price on the Dow Jones. There is also market distortion.

"Market distortion is caused by government taxation policy. Most governments give beneficial tax rates to capital gains, as opposed to interest. This is because of the risk involved in capital gains. Rational investors willing to put their money at risk would completely eschew capital investments if their gains from that investment were taxed as income. If the tax rate for the risky equity is the same as the secure bond investment, why take a chance on buying Bank of Montreal shares when you can buy the bonds and be guaranteed your income every year? The taxation authorities regard bond interest as riskless, and therefore tax it as if it was employment income. The average investor knows that if a dollar is made in interest, the investor gets to keep only 60 cents. That same gross profit in the equity market will translate into 73 cents after tax. Regrettably, that thinking has followed most investors into their untaxed pension-savings strategy, and is perpetuated by the equity-fund managers. The fund managers benefit from maintaining this thought process, since they get twice the fee income from managing equity funds that they do for bond funds."

With my accountant's background, I still wanted a hard number — something you could believe in. "Okay, Ang, what number should I use as a benchmark when considering equity markets?" I asked.

"A good yardstick, according to economic theory, would be 6 percent compounded annually for the U.S. market, after inflation. This fits in with the growth in the U.S. index of industrial production of about 4 percent compounded annually."

"Wait a minute. I've seen 14-percent one-year growth numbers for the market indices in recent years."

"Remember what I said about the 1930s, 1940s, and 1970s? A decade or two of negative or minimal numbers can quickly erode the effect of a few years at 14 percent."

I finally had a firm number. Ang used more escape clauses than a corporate lawyer. I now understood why he had been a success in the investment business.

"Okay, I agree. Let's say the investor can count on a 4-percent long-term growth in the index of industrial production, with a multiplier effect giving rise to a real 6-percent growth in equity prices. Now what about the bond market?"

"The best study I saw covered the U.S. bond market from 1924 to 1964. In that period, the highest-rated bonds (that is, best quality) gave a real return of 4 percent. However, the lowest-rated bonds gave another 1.5 points of yield, for a grand total of 5.5 percent compounded annually."

"Well, I wouldn't want to own those lower-rated ones, so I guess the number is 4-percent growth in the bond market," I said.

"Stewart, you can't make a statement like that until you have all the facts. The failure rate in the lower-rated bonds over that period was only 4 percent, and even then, the holders of those bonds would have received some return of their capital when the failed firms' assets were sold in bankruptcy. The odds that you would hold all those 4-percent losers is pretty slim. As well, note that the time span under study included the Great Depression. In the most recent 40 years, the failure rate of the lower-rated bonds has been less than 3 percent."

"Yeah, I guess the odds of finding the 3-percent losers are less than buying shares in the Bre-X mining scam. So I could settle for the 5.5-percent growth rate in the bond market."

At this point I hauled out my trusty pocket financial calculator, blew the paint dust off it, and looked at the return on a $5,000 investment, made each year over 30 years, at 6 percent (the equity return) and 5.5 percent (the bond return). The difference was just $33,000. Boy, did I feel like a dummy. By giving up a mere $1,100 a year over the past 30 years, I could have grown my self-directed pension plan at 5.5 percent with no worries.

Here are what my calculations looked like:

Investment	Return
Invest $5,000 per year for 30 years at 6%	$395,290
Invest $5,000 per year for 30 years at 5.5%	$362,177
Difference	$33,113

I could have called the $1,100-a-year portfolio insurance. What was even more discouraging was the fact that the mutual-fund salespeople always showed me the return on the indices, seldom on their funds. In reality, if I were to hold a mutual fund over that period of time, my return would be less because I would have had to pay trading costs and management fees. Ang babbled on about the various growth rates, but I now was intrigued by the bond market.

"That's kind of theoretical, Ang. You are showing me numbers based on no inflation. What happens in the real world? I hear bonds take a beating during inflation."

"Stewart, it really gets confusing when you have to factor in inflation. Another way of looking at the two market returns is their actual yield to the investor. Most Canadians think in terms of their Registered Retirement Savings Plans, which have to be invested primarily in Canadian securities. One of Canada's long-time bond dealers, Scotia Capital Markets, conducted an interesting study recently. It looked at what you would have made, after all was said and done, by investing in the bond market and the Toronto Stock Exchange Composite Index of 300 shares over various holding periods, thus representing typical RRSP investors. I have that graph somewhere here in my pocket."

Performance of Stocks Versus Bonds

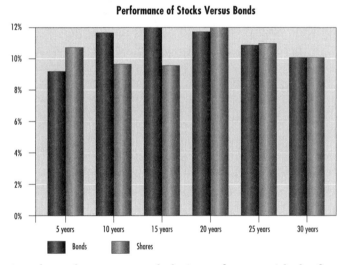

Angelo took out a crumpled piece of paper with the figures shown below.

Most retirees have invested their pension money over a 15- to 30-year period. Recent experience indicates they should have been in the bond market. If you factor in the higher fees for equity mutual funds, bond investors substantially outperform their equity counterparts.

Another consideration, I realized, is where you had invested that money. It was no wonder that the Europeans preferred bonds to shares. Their share markets had lousy performance statistics. The U.S. stock market seemed to have the best and most consistent growth rate; there the investor had an even chance of making somewhere around 6-percent real growth.

I was still thinking about whether or not the minuscule higher performance of equities over bonds — about 1.5 percent — justified the risk of owning shares, when we arrived at the trattoria. The place was fairly full, and I found myself listening to French at the table behind us and German beside us.

"What is this? A tourist trap?" I inquired from Ang.

"No, just popular with the yachties you see around the various yards working on their boats or, in the case of those bigger yachts, watching the work being done."

"Hey, I see they have a clam appetizer on the menu. Are those like the littlenecks?"

"No. They are about the size of a 25-cent coin, cooked in wine and butter, and very fattening. Sarah always complains when I order them, and then eats more than half the plate. Go for it."

I did. I also ordered a veal chop stuffed with Gorgonzola cheese. This was accompanied by a bottle of Barbaresco and finished off with a zabaglione. The zabaglione was prepared at the table. The waiter wheeled over a little cart with an alcohol burner and a pot with a round bottom. He then broke three egg yolks into the pot and began to stir it with a whisk. As the egg yolks began to froth, he added Marsala wine and brown sugar — simple, but effective. Sort of like the bond market. I pointed this out to Angelo, at which point the previous French speakers addressed us in English and asked what we knew about the bond market. They were a couple from Montreal who, after having read *Take Your Money and Run!*, had left Canada and were now cruising the Mediterranean.

5

Of Human Bondage

The French Canadian couple were named Gaston and Michelle. Yachties being a gregarious bunch, there was no question that they would slide their chairs over and dig into the conversation. They had heard us talking about bonds and wanted to know how the bond market worked. In fact, they didn't know what a bond was. They had been civil servants all their lives, but after having read *Take Your Money and Run!* they ran off to Ireland, became resident there, and then took out their Registered Retirement Savings Plan pension money. After paying 15-percent withholding tax to the Government of Canada, they invested all their funds in Swiss annuities. This had me confused.

"Why," I asked, "would you pay tax on taking out your RRSPs to Ireland when you could have rolled them over into Canadian annuities for free in Canada?"

"Gaston was worried about the protection our annuity

would have in Canada. It seems the government is allowing people's retirement money to be taken away from them. As well, having paid the withholding tax, we receive all our annuity payouts tax free from the Swiss insurance company. It doesn't matter where we go; our payments come to us gross, and then it is up to the taxing authorities to try to get the money. They are never excited about doing that. Gaston knows from his days in government that they like to have the money up front, and then let you try to get it back," Michelle replied.

"If you've got annuity income, why do you want to learn about bonds?" Angelo inquired.

"Because of our highly taxed, frugal lifestyle in Canada, we came away unprepared for tax-free living, and every year we have some money left over to invest."

Angelo bellowed, "Leftovers? You have money left over? In the words of Andrew Carnegie, 'The man who dies thus rich dies disgraced.'"

"Ang, settle down. I'm sure it's just a momentary lapse. Why not tell the folks what you know about bonds?"

⌐

It turned out that our new friends knew nothing about the bond market. Angelo had to explain that bonds are essentially IOUs issued by companies or governments.

"To be classed as a bond rather than a debenture," Angelo explained, "the loan has to be backed by some collateral. In the early days when governments borrowed money, it was for capital expenditures, so there was always some asset underlying the loan. As such, government borrowing was done in the form of bonds. Later, the government stopped backing the debt with assets, but the instruments still continued to be known as bonds.

"Debentures, on the other hand, are general obligations to pay and are un-collateralized. So a company will offer its good credit as the underlying pledge to pay the interest and principal when due. Instead of seeking money from a bank, the borrower gets it from the public at large."

Gaston said, "The company or government then issues a cheque for the interest and pays you the loan amount back at the end of the loan. Correct?"

"Not exactly," Ang replied. "If the borrower is a government, it will keep a list of the people it owes money to under the terms of a bond indenture and pay them directly. A company will use the services of a trustee. The trustee will record the names of the people owed money and, every six months, will collect the interest from the company and pay it out to the bondholders. When a bondholder sells his or her position, the new owner notifies the trustee and the interest payments are redirected."

"How do these bonds originate?" Michelle asked.

"In the case of government bonds, the government's finance department will discuss with the brokerage community how much money it intends to raise, and together they determine an interest rate that will make the bonds attractive to investors. The brokerage companies form a syndicate to buy the bonds from the government and then resell them.

"A company seeking funds will approach a brokerage firm, and if the brokers believe that the company can support the debt and that the brokers can sell the debenture to investors, a deal is struck. The debentures or bonds are priced and then sold to the investment community."

"My broker has never called me offering bonds," said Gaston.

"I am not surprised," Angelo continued, "because the usual customers for these issues are pension funds, who buy them in $100,000 tranches. Unlike Europe, the retail market for bonds has been slow to develop in North America. The dealers are reluctant to trade in small amounts, and the public has been largely unaware of bonds. The retail market has also been hindered by the availability of government savings bonds aimed at the retail market. These have such low interest rates that they turn off the small investor."

"Angelo was telling me earlier," I said to our new friends, "that bonds had, under some conditions, a slightly lower return to the investor after tax than did equities. Perhaps, Angelo, you, will explain now why pension funds are so keen to own bonds?"

"They are keen, Stewart, to the extent that most pension funds hold somewhere near 70 percent of their investments in fixed-income securities, such as bonds and mortgages. This is because pension funds go untaxed until distributed."

"Of course," I said. I had completely forgotten that pension funds are untaxed accounts. "Therefore, a bond must be the perfect investment vehicle for a pension fund."

"Not quite," Angelo replied. "There is the liquidity dilemma."

At this point, there was a language problem: our French-speaking friends had interpreted this to mean we had run out of wine. They immediately ordered a bottle of Refosco, and the conversation lost its previous direction and headed for new topics. My companions spent the next hour discussing the merits and drawbacks of full-battened mainsails. The yachties left soon after, but not before inviting us for dinner the following evening at another trattoria they knew of.

"You really captivated our new friends," I said. "It must be the gift of the gab."

"Yeah, some people account for my verbosity with the suspicion that there must have been an Irish priest in the family's long, Italian bloodline."

6

The New, Improved Credit Crunchy

I had bought a box of Monte Cristo Number 2s at the duty-free shop in Amsterdam on the way over, so Ang and I puffed our way home through the streets of Viareggio like a couple of steam engines.

"Back in the trattoria, you mentioned liquidity as a problem with bonds," I said. "What did you mean by that?"

"If you sell a $100-million issue in million-dollar tranches, you've only got 100 holders of the paper, so there are only that many people who know about the security. When it comes time for one of those holders to sell, there are not many people around interested in the security."

"But if you are talking about a million-dollar trade, there have to be some pretty good commission bucks in that," I said. "Enough to generate interest, at least."

"Stewart, bonds are not sold on a commission basis. They are traded net to the customer. So if you were to step out to buy a Cambridge Shopping Centres 8-percent debenture, you would find in the paper that the bond was being offered at, say, $101, and bid $99. You would probably pay $101, and the dealer would have sold you something for which he paid par or, in other words, $100. He therefore makes a point on the bond."

"But I thought bonds were denominated in $1,000 units."

"They are. You can seldom find a $100 denomination, although some have been issued. In reality, when a bond dealer says a bond is selling at $101, what he means is that the price for a $1,000 par certificate is $1,010."

"Boy, that's rich, Ang. The guy is making a 1-percent commission, especially if he can go out and bid $99.5."

"Stew, you've raised a number of issues. First, the dealer is not making a commission. When you receive your contract, it will show you the price you paid for the bond and the amount of accrued interest you purchased. The vendor of the bond demands payment of the interest earned, but not paid out, from the time of the last interest payment to the date you begin to accrue the interest. There will be no mention of commission. As well, the contract will specify that the dealer sold you the bond as a principal, not as an agent. That means the dealer owned the bond when it was sold to you, unlike a share of stock, which the broker sells to you as an agent on behalf of a client.

"Second, the bond business was once the most profitable end of the securities business. Look at what happens. A bond syndicate buys from the government a tranche of bonds with a 6-percent coupon for $1,000 apiece. Bond interest accrues daily. If you own a bond for one day and sell it, the purchaser of the bond includes in his payment the interest you earned for the day you owned it. Remember, too, that the shorter the term of the loan, the lower the interest rate. The cheapest loan you can arrange is overnight. So let's say that the cost of overnight money is 3 percent. The syndicate members go to the bank and borrow overnight money at 3 percent, and earn interest on the bond inventory at 6 percent. While the bonds are in inventory, the dealer is making money on the 3-percentage-point spread between his cost of borrowing and the interest he is making on the security. If he can then sell the bond at $100.5, he scores again. Then there is the secondary market. That is even richer."

"By the secondary market, you mean trading in the security after it has been distributed from an underwriting, correct?"

"Yeah. What usually happens is that the firm heading the syndicate that underwrote the bonds takes on the role of running a secondary market, in which it offers to buy at one price and sell at a slightly higher price. The trader responsible for that particular security will adjust the price spreads, depending on the volume of bonds being offered and sought."

"Isn't that risky?" I asked.

"Only when you have an inverted yield curve, which means short-term money costs you more than long-term money. This seldom happens, but when it does, it can destroy a firm caught off guard, as happened to A.E. Ames in the late 1970s. At the time, A.E. Ames was one of the largest bond and security firms in Canada. The interest cost of carrying the firm's inventory was more than the interest it earned."

"Ang, I don't understand what you mean by an inverted yield curve. That sounds like it's upside down."

"It is. Let me show you." Ang sketched out the following graphs.

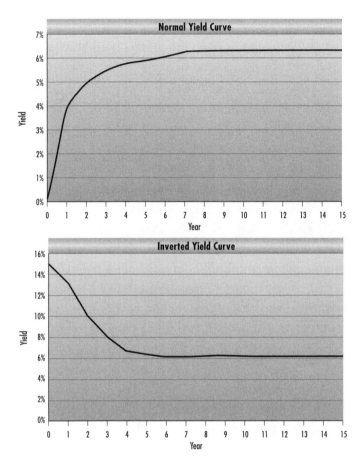

"Look at the typical or ordinary yield curve. As the period of the loan (shown along the bottom axis) increases, the interest charged (shown on the vertical axis) increases. That seems intuitively correct. But when a nation's economy gets overheated, the value of its currency falls, or there appears to be inflation coming into the economy, the government will act to restrict the availability of money. Besides raising what is called the fed rate in the United States, or the discount rate in Canada — the rate at which the chartered banks can borrow from the central bank — the government can affect the availability of money in other ways. The best way to do this is to offer investors very high rates of interest. Your bank, when faced with the prospect of lending you money at 8 percent or investing in a treasury bill for 12 percent, will obviously choose the bill. When the bank gives the government a million dollars to buy a short-term treasury certificate, that money goes out of circulation. As money becomes scarce, its rental cost, known to you as interest, goes up. Only borrowers with very high rates of return can afford to borrow, and the yield curve takes on this shape.

"Obviously, you get a better return for lending short term than you do for the longer term. There have been periods like this at the end of every economic boom when the government puts the brakes on the economy by increasing short-term rates. What happens to the pension-fund investors is that, with short-term rates in the double digits, they can abandon the vagaries of the stock market and invest in certainty with a high return."

"I get it," I said. "The second graph is just the first one upside down. I would suspect, as well, that it is very difficult to sell a long-term bond issue when the short rates are high."

It was obvious to me that, in an environment where borrowing costs from the bank were 15 percent, you would not be buying inventory that yielded 10 percent. But I now knew how bonds were born. Some entity wanted to borrow money, and a syndicate was set up by financiers to borrow that money from the investors. The investors received a bond certificate as an IOU, attesting to the borrowers' indebtedness. The lead firm of the syndicate would operate an aftermarket so that the holders of the certificates could sell them, and those who did not participate in the primary, or original, issue might be able to buy them. That all seemed simple enough. I left Ang at the entrance to the boatyard with the promise that I would return to boat-bottom scraping in the morning.

What a way to live — a great meal, a sound education, and a cigar to top it off.

7

The Value of Time

I rolled out of bed and into a bright sunny morning. I stopped for a coffee and pastry at the local coffee bar on my way to the boatyard.

Angelo was already working when I arrived. I then recognized my folly. Angelo's boat was a full-keeled Hans Christian ketch. The underside was adorned not with a little fin sticking down from the hull, but with a full-length keel from bow to rudder. It all had to be cleaned of its old bottom paint, right down to the bare gelcoat. I had not made a wise offer.

I greeted Ang and asked him where he wanted me to start. As I started to scrape, I said, "Ang, your firm was in the bond business. You should have made enough money to hire somebody to do this for you."

"It wasn't as easy as you make it out to be. Remember what I said: the bond syndicate buys the bonds. It actually owns inventory. This is very unlike share underwriting, which in most cases is not an underwriting at all. With shares, the brokerage firm acts as an agent and sells the shares on a best-effort basis on behalf of the company's treasury, the owner of the shares. In other words, the investment firm is selling the new shares as the issuer's agent. If they don't sell, the issuing corporation still owns them. With bonds, if they don't sell, the brokerage owns them because they bought them from the issuer. There were a number of times when we were stuck with unsold inventory on the shelf, which we eventually sold at a loss."

"Angelo, you said that the inventory had a positive carry, in that the interest earned would more than offset the interest paid on the money borrowed to buy the issue. How could you lose money?"

"Let me give you an example. Many years ago, we participated in a syndicate that bought the bonds of a forest-products company from its treasury. While we were in distribution, a forest-products analyst at one of the non-participating brokerages came out with a negative report on the industry, outlining the likelihood of much lower prices for pulp and paper. The sentiment towards the industry went from positive to negative before we could unload all the bonds. We had a positive carry for a short period, and then the dollar started to weaken and the government bumped up short-term interest rates to support the dollar. This not only further depressed the price of our inventory, but pushed us into a negative spread on our borrowing costs, versus the coupon on the bonds. Our loss on the tag end of the issue more than offset the gain we made on the bulk."

"That sounds scary," I said. "Did it happen often?"

"Often enough. You see, the margin on bond deals is skimpy to start with, especially now that the banks are in the business and the competition fierce. The money is made in leading the syndicate and selling a high volume. But when interest rates go up and borrowers flee, there is little new business to be done. The trading in previously issued bonds dries up because no one wants to sell at a loss."

"Whoa, slow down," I said. "You're starting to confuse me. You said interest rates went up, and inventory and business prices declined. Could you explain?"

"Ah yes, the coupon-versus-yield question, " Angelo said, "the very essence of the bond market. Understand that, and you know everything.

"A bond is issued at a fixed interest rate; however, the yield to the investors can vary depending on the price they pay for it. Let's work, for example, with a $1,000 bond issued with a 10-percent coupon. The interest rate is called a coupon, because bonds were originally issued in bearer form. In other words, unregistered. Whoever held the physical bond actually owned it and the interest due. These bonds have almost completely disappeared, because the government fears the loss of taxation with something so easily negotiable. Because the bond was unregistered, the issuer would have no way of sending the bondholder the interest when due. So the bonds were issued with a coupon attached for each interest period. When the date on the coupon was reached, the bondholder would clip the coupon from the certificate, take it to the bank, and receive cash. It was like a postdated cheque. When the bonds matured, the bondholders took them to a bank and received their principal. The bank then returned the paper to the corporation or government and received its money. Now, let's say that a government bond was issued for 20 years with a 10-percent coupon."

Ang continued by scribbling the following formula down for me. "Look, if you bought the bond for $1,000, a year before it matured, your yield would be:—

$$\text{Yield} = \frac{\text{Interest received}}{\text{Principal}} = \frac{\$100}{\$1,000} = 10\%$$

However, if you bought that bond for $950, your yield would be:

$$\text{Yield} = \frac{\$100}{\$950} = 10.53\%$$

"These numbers represent your simple, or cash, yield. However, in a year's time you will also receive the principal amount of the bond, which is $1,000, even though you paid only $950 for it. Therefore, your yield to maturity would be:

$$\text{Yield} = \frac{\$100 \text{ (interest)} + \$50 \text{ (recoup of discount)}}{\$950} = 15.79\%$$

"As you can see, when a bond sells for an amount other than its principal of $1,000, the investor's yield to maturity changes, since the total amount of money received changes. In this case, the price went down and the yield therefore went up. Coupons are fixed, so a 10-percent bond will always pay $100. The prices at which bonds trade are not, thus varying the yield. If the price of a bond goes up, the divisor in the equation above increases, thereby shrinking the figure for the yield. Obviously, if you buy a bond at a premium over its par value of $1,000, you are going to lose a bit of that premium every year as the bond approaches maturity and par, thus reducing your yield to maturity."

"Why would a bond sell at a premium?" I asked.

"Stewart, if U.S. government bonds are being issued with a 5-percent coupon today, how much would you pay for an older bond with a 10-percent coupon?"

"I'd have to pay the current owner more than par to get him to part with his higher coupon paper."

"What you would discover in this instance is that the erosion of the premium over the life of the bond being subtracted from that higher coupon would bring your yield to maturity to the current interest rate (5 percent), although the coupon rate is 10 percent."

"That seems logical," I said, "but the calculations must be hell."

"Many years ago, bond traders worked with books that would price a bond based on a yield to maturity. Bond traders would look in their books with a yield in mind to find a price for a bond with a stated period to maturity, at a prescribed coupon. Now that calculation is done on hand-held calculators. Let me show you how time affects that premium."

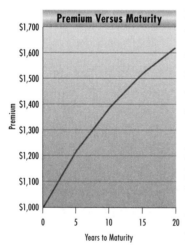

Premium Versus Maturity

At this point, Angelo used his chisel to scratch a chart that looked like this one on the bottom of the boat through the old paint. As he explained it, if you are buying a 10-percent bond with a year to maturity, when the current interest rate is 5 percent, you are willing to pay for the extra amount of interest from the current bondholder.

"A currently issued 5-percent bond is going to give you $50 in interest in a year's time. The older 10-percent bond is going to give you $100. What would you pay someone for that extra $50 to be received in a year's time if the current interest rate is 5 percent? You would pay $47.62 for that extra $50. Therefore, the total cost to you would be:

Principal amount discounted at 5%	$952.38
$50 coupon interest discounted back at 5%	$47.62
Extra interest $50 interest discounted	$47.62
Total	$1,047.62

"So, if you were to buy the 10-percent coupon bond in a 5-percent interest environment, and it had only a year to maturity, you'd pay the current owner $1,047.62 for the $1,100 you would receive in a year's time. What kind of yield would you achieve?

Amount received	$1,100.00
Amount paid (investment)	$1,047.62
Net to you	$52.38
Original investment	$1,047.62
Yield = $52.38 ÷ $1,047.62 =	5%

"The extra interest you are going to receive is discounted to reflect that it is a year away. Obviously, the more extra interest to be received, the higher the price of the bond — but always discounted back to today's value. As the chart shows, if you were to buy a 10-percent bond when rates are 5 percent, you would pay in excess of $1,600 for a 20-year bond (with forty semi-annual payments outstanding), but only $1,400 for a bond with only ten years of life left (or twenty semi-annual payments due to you)."

That night, I did the calculations and they looked like this:

Year	Current Value	Cum. Value	Bond Price
1	$47.62	$47.62	$1,047.62
2	45.35	92.97	1,092.97
3	43.19	136.16	1,136.16
4	41.14	177.30	1,177.30
5	39.17	216.47	1,216.47
6	37.31	253.78	1,253.78
7	35.54	289.32	1,289.32
8	33.84	323.16	1,323.16
9	32.23	355.39	1,355.39
10	30.70	386.09	1,386.09

What struck me was the deteriorating present value of the extra coupon in future years. This was to come back to me later, when Angelo started talking about strips. But first we had to cover the basics.

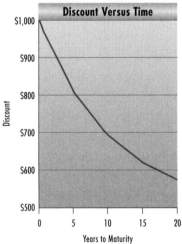

Discount Versus Time
(Discount / Years to Maturity)

"What does the other side of the equation look like?" I asked.

"If you mean a bond that has a lower coupon than to-day's rates, it looks like this." Again, Angelo used his chisel as a scribe and the bottom of his boat as a palette.

"With interest rates at 10 per-cent, you could buy a 5-percent-coupon bond with 20 years to maturity for about $590. The effect you would experience is a yield of 10 percent to maturity. Obviously, with a ten-year bond, the wait to get to par is shorter, and therefore the discount for having to hold it is less. As such, the bond with a ten-year maturity would be priced around $680."

"Ang, this gets kind of scary. If I paid a premium to buy a 10-percent coupon bond when rates were 5 percent, its price would decline if rates started to move up."

"Precisely. And the longer the maturity of the bond you were holding, the greater would be your loss."

"What kind of numbers are we looking at?" I asked.

"If you climb the ladder and look in the cabin, you will find a bond calculator on my chart table."

"Why do I have to go up the ladder?"

"You asked the question."

It's about twelve feet from the ground to the top of the gunwale on Ang's boat, and it seemed I was always the one going up to fetch. But I was curious. I'd heard of bond traders' making and losing big money, and I had always wondered how. I grabbed a couple of beers and climbed down the ladder once again. I handed Angelo his calculator and a Moretti beer. As he punched out the numbers on his calculator, he again drew a graph on the old, anti-fouling paint. The horizontal axis illustrated the level of prevailing interest rates and the vertical axis charted the price of a 20-year bond if those rates prevailed.

"Now look at this," he said. "The bond with the 10-percent coupon and 20 years to maturity would sell for $2,300 at a current interest rate of 2 percent. As you get closer to a 10-percent current rate, the price drops to par. Mind you, the person holding a 5-percent coupon security would see his

Price of 0%, 5%, and 10% 20-Year Bonds at Various Current Rates

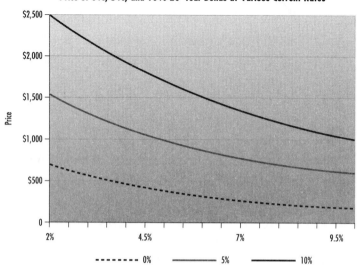

20-year bond priced at $570 at a 10-percent current rate. At the end of their lives, the bonds are going to be redeemed at par, or $1,000. The difference between what you pay is the premium or discount, which will give you a yield equivalent to that of a new issue sold at par with the current interest rate as a coupon."

"If I understand you correctly, the price I pay for a previously issued bond that has an interest rate different from current rates will depend on whether the coupon attached to the old bond is lower or higher than the rates being paid on currently issued bonds."

"Correct."

"I see," I said. "There's no free lunch at the bond market. If I buy a bond with a higher coupon than those currently being issued, I'll pay a premium that will, in effect, lower my yield to current rates. It stands to reason, then, that if I buy a bond with a lower coupon than the new bonds on offer, I'll get it at a discount that will raise its effective yield to the rates prevailing. What simple elegance! But wait a minute. What if I bought a bond when rates were 5 percent and they then rose to 10 percent in a year's time?" I asked.

"You take a kick in the head," Ang said. "Investors are not going to pay you par for your 5-percent bond when they can walk into the market and get a 10-percent yield at par."

"That's painful."

"Is it? What if you have no intention of selling any part of your bond portfolio? Would you care what the value is then? Price is only important if you intend to buy or sell. I had a difficult time convincing my stockbroker of this. He would call me and say, 'Ang, your portfolio is falling like a stone.' I would ask him if the bonds were still paying their interest and, if they were, not to bother calling me. I had not bought the bonds to trade them, but to get a return on my investment. Later, I'd get a call about how my portfolio was heading for the sky. Interest rates were falling and I was getting richer by the minute. Was I? No, because if I sold any of my now high-priced bonds, I would have to replace them with other high-priced bonds. So I told him, 'No more calls, please.'"

"There must be somebody trading bonds," I said. "I've read about bond traders making or losing fortunes for their firms."

"There is a lively secondary market in bonds, because at any point in time there are investors who want to change the maturity of their portfolios, who have received cash, or who are in need of cash. Let me give you an example of two traders.

"Now, let's say these two traders figure interest rates are going to fall from 10 percent to 2 percent. Let's look at the chart I showed you illustrating the price of different coupon bonds at different rates:

Price of 0%, 5%, and 10% 20-Year Bonds at Various Current Rates

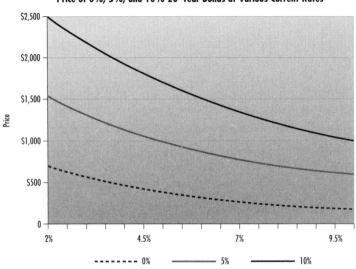

The person who buys the low-coupon bond is going to triple his money as the bond goes from $570 to $1,500. The person who buys the high coupon bond is only going to make two and one-half times his money. You see, Stewart, when interest rates go down, everybody makes money, but the person holding the low-coupon bonds makes the most. Look at the holder of a zero-coupon bond. That person's price goes from $142 to $671. Nobody makes money when interest rates are going up, because bond prices will be falling. However, the holder of high-coupon bonds loses less."

"So that's what bond trading is about: speculating on the direction of interest rates."

"Precisely. But the bond market is much larger than the stock market, and trading can become frantic. Especially when you consider that with top-grade bonds, you only need to put up 10 percent of the value of the bond. So with a million dollars, you can trade 10-million-dollars' worth. Look what happens to a 5-percent coupon bond when yields fall from 5 percent to 4.5 percent. The price changes by 7 percent. So if you put up a million dollars, levering it to hold 10-million-dollars' worth of bonds, and make the right call on interest rates, you could make $700,000. That is a 70-percent return on your original million-dollar investment, and it could happen overnight. It is because of the size of the market and the price changes that there is such liquidity. There are a lot of players. People like you and me would be foolish to step into speculating in that market. However, the trading ensures that there is lots of liquidity in the top-grade, big-issue bonds. Remember what we said earlier about the premium or discount on bonds with coupons different from the current yields. The longer the term to maturity, the greater the price differential from par. Therefore, the real cowboys in the bond-trading pit, those who place bets on rates, go for the longest possible maturities."

"What does all this mean to me?" I asked.

"I've told you how bond prices are determined. You asked."

"I'm sure that you could have told me without scraping all that paint off."

"Yeah, but I kind of like the idea of killing a lot of birds with a few stones. After all, I am not here to lecture on the bond market. I am here to refinish my hull," Ang said.

"All you had to say was that a low-coupon, long-maturity bond will increase more in value during a falling interest-rate regime, but lose more in price during a period of increasing interest rates."

"Yeah, well what about high-coupon bonds?" Ang retorted.

"Simple. The higher the coupon, the less the bond will fall during a rising-interest scenario. But doesn't maturity affect the price of bonds in a changing interest-rate environment?" I asked. "I would have thought that when rates fall, bond buyers will pay more to lock in a longer stream of high-interest payments than they would for just a few."

"More bloody questions! Let's have some lunch instead," Ang said.

I really wanted lunch, as I had seen some of the wonderful panini, or Italian sandwiches, being put together at a trattoria just outside the boatyard. But I was also hungry for more knowledge. I only had Ang for a couple of days, since we were expecting our wives back soon, and then it would be back to Toronto.

"Look," I said. "If you draw another chart on the hull, think of the paint we will have removed."

"If I didn't know better, I'd think you were conning me. Okay, let's look at the maturity question. You are correct. In a falling-interest-rate scenario, you would pay more for a longer stream of high payments than a short one. Conversely, in a rising-interest-rate environment, the longer you are stuck with a low-coupon flow, the worse off you are. Let me show you."

At this, more paint flew off the bottom of the boat, and I was presented with something resembling this graph.

Ang continued. "What this shows is that if current rates are 5 percent, and you want to buy an existing five-year bond with a 10-percent coupon, you would pay $1,218, whereas for a zero-coupon bond of five-year maturity you would only pay $781. In both cases, your yield to maturity would be 5 percent. Looking at the 20-year scenario, your zero-coupon

Prices of 0%, 5%, and 10% Coupon Bonds ot 5% Current Rates

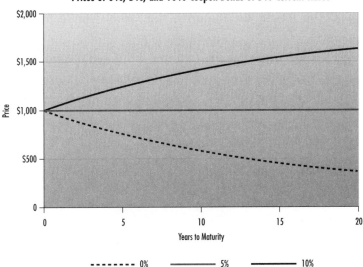

bond only costs you $372. Your yield of 5 percent is made up of the recapture of the discount over time, since you will be paid par ($1,000) for the bond when the time to maturity becomes zero. Note that in each year approaching maturity, the price of the zero coupon goes up.

"In the case of the 10-percent coupon bond, when prevailing rates are 5 percent, your actual yield is reduced from the 10-percent coupon you receive by the amount of premium that is lost annually to take you down to current yields. Each year, as the bond gets closer to maturity, its value decreases until par is reached when the bond is surrendered."

I noticed that with a 5-percent coupon bond, the price would not change over time if current rates stayed at 5 percent.

Angelo and I headed off for lunch while my mind churned with the intricacies of bond pricing. I concluded that high-coupon bonds gave you the best insurance against fluctuating rates. The longer the maturity, the more volatile the price changes.

When we arrived at the trattoria, I ordered a sandwich of Gorgonzola cheese, roasted red peppers, and prosciutto. If you think sex is great, try that sandwich sometime.

8

The Stripper in the Junkyard

As we were walking back to the boatyard, I saw a French-built sailboat being towed to the slipway for lifting. It was a wreck. When I pointed it out to Angelo, he said, "Oh yeah, a charter boat. Within a short period of use, those boats look worse than Chinese junks."

"Speaking of junk," I said, "what is a junk bond?"

"For some people, a junk bond is at the very lowest end of the bond-rating scale. For others it is simply an unrated bond."

"What do they do, hold beauty contests for bonds? Who is the judge?"

"There are two big bond-rating services out of the U.S., Standard & Poor's and Moody's, and one out of Canada, the Dominion Bond Rating Service. These services examine the credit worthiness of most of the major issuers. As well, most national jurisdictions have one or more bond-rating agencies. They assess an issuer's ability to earn the interest necessary, as well as the likelihood that the issuer will pay the principal at maturity. The balance sheet, income statement, and prospects for the company are thoroughly reviewed before the issue is priced. This assessment is used to price the paper on a yield basis. The higher the risk, the higher the yield the investors will expect. That greater yield is obtained by either selling the bond at less than par or adjusting the interest rate up to meet the lender's risk perception. If the credit agencies refuse to give a bond a rating, it is immediately classed as junk."

"Why would anyone buy a junk bond?" I asked.

"Everything in life has a price. The vendors will keep demanding extra value for the investors until the underwriter achieves a package that will sell."

"Could you explain that?"

"Say a new issuer, let's call it Internet Industries, wants to raise $50 million to expand its business. The bond underwriter will look at the company, its assets, and business and may conclude that even with a 2-percent-interest premium over existing corporate yields, the issue would be hard to sell. Remember that the underwriter is going to buy the issue from the company and sell it to the public. It has to be attractive to buyers, or the underwriter will be stuck with it. If the interest rate is raised further, the company might have difficulty servicing the debt — the interest charges could cripple it. If the price is dropped too low, the investors might get frightened away or it may not raise enough money to accommodate the issuer. How can it be made appealing? The usual answer is to give the investors a bonus in the form of an attached warrant, which allows the investors to buy shares of the company at a discount over time or gives them the right to convert the bond into common shares at a specified price, higher than the current share price. If the 'sweetener' added to the bond is attractive enough, the buyers will take the package."

I was impressed. The market had something for everyone. The idea of having a "call" on the shares of a company and, at the same time, earning interest sounded like the best of all worlds to me. I asked Angelo why all bonds weren't issued as convertibles.

"The convertible feature is an extra for the buyer and an escape for the issuer. If the company had wanted to issue common shares in the first instance, it would have done so, but it also might not have been able to. However, in this case, management believes that it can take on the liability of debt and survive until the time when the shares are higher priced. It provides the equity inducement to either make the issue more saleable, or to provide a share issuance in the future."

I was confused. We seemed to be talking about both a share and a debenture issue at the same time. I pointed this out to Angelo.

"The management at Internet Industries sees its shares trading at $5 each and believes they are easily worth $10. If it does a $50-million, 8-percent convertible-debenture issue, redeemable on June 30, 2010, with each $1,000 par being convertible into 100 shares, then the conversion price of the shares is $10 each. If the $50 million raised improves the profitability of the company, the shares might trade to $15. At this point, the debenture holders would convert their debt into equity, and the company, in effect, would have issued five-million shares at $10 each, with no underwriting fees — and would have dispensed of the liability of the $50-million loan. It is as though it issued shares at $10 each to cover the loan, something it could not do earlier. The call feature you see with convertibles is there to force conversion. The convertible usually gives the company the right to call the bonds for redemption at par when the shares are trading at 120 percent or more of the conversion price. If the shares were priced higher than the conversion price, the bondholder would see his bonds trading at a premium and would have to be terminally stupid to accept redemption at par over conversion for more money. As with all specialized areas, this one has developed its own jargon," Ang said, scribbling something. "Let's look at the definitions using our fictitious company, Internet Industries."

Internet Industries	
Coupon	8 percent
Maturity	June 30, 2010
Conversion Ratio	100
Conversion Price	$10
Conversion Value	= Conversion Ratio x Market Share Price
Conversion Premium ($)	= Debenture Price − (Market Share Price x Conversion Ratio)
Conversion Premium (%)	= Conversion Premium ($) ÷ Conversion Value
Payback	= Conversion Premium ($) ÷ (Interest Amount − Dividend)

"If we ascribe some values to the fictitious bond and share, we can calculate some of the numbers above."

Bond Price	=	$980.00
Share Price	=	$7.50
Annual Interest	=	$80.00

"With those numbers, the conversion value, which is calculated by multiplying the conversion ratio by the share price, works out to $750. The bond cannot trade below this price, otherwise arbitragers would buy the bond, convert it into shares, and sell them at a profit.

"The conversion premium, in dollars, is the amount obtained by subtracting the conversion value from the bond price. In this instance, the difference is $230.

"The value most often seen in the financial press is the conversion premium, expressed as a percentage. This is obtained by dividing the dollar-conversion premium by the conversion value. In this case, it is $230 divided by $750, or, when expressed as a percentage, 31 percent.

"The payback is an expression of how long it will take to get your money back if you paid a premium over the conversion value. Seeing as our company pays no dividend, the calculation is simplified to the conversion premium divided by the annual interest. For our example, that works out to $230 divided by $80, or 2.9 years."

"That sounds like a lot of arithmetic to buy a bond," I said.

"Stewart, you're an accountant. It shouldn't be that tough for you — or a grade-six mathematics student."

"Ease up on the abuse. And don't dust off that old saw that 'accountants are just economists with personality,' which is patently untrue."

"Stew, are you denying that accountants have personality?"

"They have more personality than renegade financiers," I said.

"That was really a low blow," Ang retorted. "For that, I might just not warn you about the pain of conversion."

"Are you talking religious or debenture?" I asked.

"Very funny. But you should be aware that when you convert a debenture, you lose the accumulated interest to that date. Therefore, unless forced into conversion, your best strategy is to convert the bond the day after the interest is paid."

"What if you're afraid the share price will fall before you can convert?" I asked.

"That's simple. Sell short* the number of shares represented by the debenture, wait until the interest is paid, and then convert to cover your short sale."

"I really like the sound of convertibles. They are better than bonds with attached warrants, because the warrants expire, while the conversion option remains open. Why would anyone buy a bond with an attached warrant, rather than a convertible?"

"You have to look at the situation from the buyer's point of view. Buyers don't want to buy equity. They want yield. Few bond investors are excited about owning common stock. If the risks are beyond what the interest rate will accommodate, though, the issuer still has to give them something attached to the bond. Look at the case of a new-issue bond with attached warrants to buy the shares of the issuer. What often happens is that, upon issue, the warrants are stripped from the bond by the purchaser and sold. By this action, the holder has reduced the cost of purchasing the bond and raised the yield further. If the bond was priced at par, and the holder was able to sell the warrants for $50, the net cost for the bond would be $950, thus obtaining a higher yield."

"So all the junkers I see out there in investorland were issued with warrants or are convertible," I replied.

---

* Short sellers sell shares they do not yet own, expecting to purchase them at a future date for delivery. In the interim, the short seller's broker will borrow shares from an existing holder to cover a demand for delivery. In this case, the short seller will convert the bond to make good on the obligation to dieliver either to the lender or the buyer. In this way, the short seller has guaranteed the sale price before receiving the shares due from conversion.

"Not necessarily, Stew. You see, not all the bonds that are currently classed as junk were issued in that class. Some bonds were issued as a good credit with a reasonable rating, but then fell into disrepute because the industry or the company lost its profitability. So not all junk bonds were born as such. Some are just fallen angels."

We arrived at the boatyard and I picked up my chisel and started scraping paint. I thought about the market for bonds compared to that for stocks. They both have their blue chips and speculative issues. It is merely a question of risk. In the case of the junk bonds, the risk is still inherently lower than that of penny stocks. I could see, however, that there are some interesting investment plays that can take place with convertibles. Then I remembered that there was a fellow in the U.S. who had made quite a fortune in junk bonds. "Angelo, who was that guy the press made all the fuss about with regard to junk bonds?" I asked.

"Oh, you mean Mike Milken. Fantastic story. Milken was working as a corporate finance officer when the U.S. government changed the investment rules for savings and loan organizations, or S&Ls, as they are called. Prior to the change, these organizations were allowed to buy only the top-rated government bonds as a parking spot for their excess funds."

"Okay, slow down again, Angelo. You're getting ahead of me. What do savings and loans do?"

"They take in deposits and lend funds out to homebuyers as mortgages. When more money comes in than can be invested in mortgages, the S&Ls have to put it in some interest-paying security to cover the interest due to their depositors. When originally instituted, the S&Ls were limited to top-grade government bonds. Then some slapheads in

Washington thought that this was too onerous a restriction, and the Senate Banking Committee changed the rules to allow investment in lower-grade securities. Milken seized on this to sell the S&Ls low-grade corporate bonds. His pitch was that there was no risk to the depositors, as the deposits were covered by government insurance. If the bonds defaulted and the S&Ls closed, the depositors would be recompensed by the government. For a while, everybody was happy. More loan capital became available for junior companies, and the S&Ls improved their interest earnings. But Milken made a mistake in allowing individual organizations to take large positions in single issues. Some of this might have been caused by the greed of the buyers. When the markets turned sour in the late 1980s, the S&Ls found that there were very low bids for the bonds they wanted to sell or, worse still, no bids. Faced with the need to pay their depositors' demands for withdrawals, and not being able to liquidate their holdings, some of them went bust. The U.S. government was now faced with a scandal of its own making and had to find a scapegoat, so it turned to the man who sold the bonds to the S&Ls. In other words, it shot the messenger. Rather than let the government prosecute his younger brother, Milken pleaded guilty to some make-believe charges, and spent three years in a country-club prison."

"It sounds to me like he was guilty of something," I said. "After all, he did sell securities to the S&Ls for which there was no market."

"You have to understand the market. When times are good, the bids for junk bonds approach or exceed par. Given a whiff of market uncertainty, the bids for low-grade securities fall more precipitously than those for blue chips, and may disappear entirely. There is a message. Don't buy junk bonds to trade; only buy to hold. The U.S. S&Ls needed liquidity, both to meet their depositors' withdrawals and for mortgage investments. The managers of the S&Ls were either greedy or stupid to buy junk bonds. Subsequently, those junk-bond portfolios appreciated in the mid-to late 1990s, in some cases going to a premium. The speculators buying those portfolios at the S&L garage sales and bankruptcy courts made fortunes. None of that was Mr. Milken's fault."

"Ang, the other thing you mentioned was a zero-coupon bond. Do companies actually issue bonds with no coupons or interest, and do people buy them?"

"Not only are they issued, but there is enough of a market that some have to be created."

"That doesn't make sense," I said. "No one is going to lend money without interest."

"How about this: lend me ten bucks and I'll pay you 11 in a year's time."

"I get it. There is an implied interest rate because you are going to pay me more than you borrowed."

"Precisely. And that is the way the U.S. treasury-bill market operates. The paper is sold to the investors at a discount and redeemed at par. The difference in the two prices is the implied interest rate. T-Bills, as they are called, are short-term. Just take that concept and extend it to ten or 20 years."

"Obviously, there are benefits and drawbacks to such paper," I said. "Tell me what they are."

"The issuers benefit because they save the cost of issuing interest cheques, and their issue expenses will be lower. Buyers benefit in so far as the interest rate is fixed, eliminating the reinvestment-rate problem. You see, Stew, when the yield to maturity is calculated on a conventional bond, the calculation assumes that the coupons received are reinvested at the determined rate. So, if you bought a bond at a time when rates were 10 percent and the dealer told you your yield to maturity was 10 percent, that calculation assumes that you would be investing the coupons you receive at 10 percent. What happens if current rates fall to 5 percent? You will never achieve your yield to maturity of 10 percent. With a zero-coupon bond, the annual increase in principal as the bond approaches maturity is considered reinvested at the yield-to-maturity rate, and because you do not receive the money until maturity there is no actual reinvesting to be done — there is no coupon — so the specified yield to maturity is achieved."

"In a time of high interest rates, that would be a real plus, Ang. If rates go down, you're still guaranteed your return. What are the disadvantages?" I asked.

"They are hard to sell and can rarely be called. As you can well imagine, having a call feature for a zero coupon would pose problems. Obviously, issuers would be reluctant to call their bonds at par before maturity, as they would pay a tremendous premium.

"Most investors, too, want a steady stream of cash flow from their bond investments to cover expenses. Zero coupons are best for professional investors, like life insurance companies and pension funds, who want to have a certain amount on hand, at a certain date, to meet a future known liability."

"Angelo, these zero coupons would be a great tax dodge, because you could continue to accrue your interest and have a tax deferral until you redeemed the bond."

"Great idea, but like so many, there are others who have

thought of it as well — in particular, the tax departments of the world. The taxing authorities of most countries will tax you on the accrued income. But for a non-taxed account, such as a pension or offshore account, these are great vehicles because they often sell at depressed prices, which give very attractive yields."

"Ang, you said a minute ago that because of their popularity, zero-coupon bonds were being created. What did you mean by that?"

"Bond dealers who see a demand for zero-coupon bonds when there's little supply create them by separating the coupons from bonds and selling each separately. This is done with previously issued provincial and federal government bonds. The dealer will take an issue with no call feature and remove the coupons. One investor will buy the coupons and another the residual, or strip. The strip is now a zero-coupon bond, and sells at a discount, to be redeemed at maturity. The coupons are also discounted to give you a present value, or purchase price."

"Give me an example," I said.

"Let's look at a recently issued 5-percent, ten-year Government of Canada bond when current rates are 5 percent. The dealer who underwrote the issue decides to turn it into a stripped bond. There are twenty coupons attached to the bond because it pays semi-annually. What are the coupons worth? The face value of each coupon is $25; however, the owner of the coupon can't get the cash for the first one for another six months, and then the rest only incrementally, every six months. Therefore, we have to discount back the value of each coupon to today. The net present value of the $500, to be received over the next ten years semi-annually, is $414.57 today."

Angelo mapped it out like this:

Payment Number	Years Hence	Present Value
1	.5	$23.84
2	1.0	$23.47
3	1.5	$23.11
4	2.0	$22.76
5	2.5	$22.41
6	3.0	$22.07
7	3.5	$21.74
8	4.0	$21.41
9	4.5	$21.09
10	5.0	$20.78
11	5.5	$20.47
12	6.0	$20.17
13	6.5	$19.88
14	7.0	$19.59
15	7.5	$19.30
16	8.0	$19.03
17	8.5	$18.76
18	9.0	$18.49
19	9.5	$18.23
20	10.0	$17.97
		TOTAL $414.57

"I can see the advantage of the strip to an insurance company or pension fund, Ang, since they would be able to lock in a yield and have the money necessary on the due date. But who would buy the coupons?" I asked.

"In the above example, you could buy $500 worth of payments for $414.57. This, in the bond trader's parlance, is a ladder, because it includes a sequence of payments — in this case, all from the same bond. So, each year, you get a fixed payment at a predetermined interest rate. Again, this would be beneficial in a non-taxed account. Assume you were a pensioner with a RRIF, an IRA, or a 401k, and you wanted to be paid out $500,000 over the next ten years, to average $50,000 per year. You would buy the ladder for $414,580 with your pension money, which would give you $500,000 of coupons, at face value. Every six months, you would have $25,000 come due, or $50,000 paid out to you each year as your retirement income."

"That is really slick," I said. "You get 5 percent on your money, and it's there when you need it, with certainty. Are there enough coupons available to allow the investor to set up any variety of plans?"

"Those avaricious stockbrokers will go out of their way to supply the market with product. If they can't find something in their inventory or on offer, they'll create it. It is a wonderful product, because a broker who started with one saleable item — a bond with twenty coupons — now has twenty coupons and one strip to sell."

"You mean that the broker might sell each coupon separately to individual buyers?"

"That is, in fact, the most common scenario," Angelo replied. "Purchasing a ladder, especially from one bond, is the exception. Suppose I wanted to pay you a balloon, or final payment, of $25,000 in five years' time I would buy 1,000 of the tenth-payment coupons for $20,780. I would then give you these coupons, and in five years' time, you could cash the coupons on their due date and receive your payment. Having a government coupon in your hand is better than a postdated cheque. If I had to issue a postdated cheque, my bank would have frozen $25,000 of my funds to ensure the funds were on deposit when due. In this case, I have tied up only $20,780 of my funds."

"But what about the income tax?" I asked. "There is an

implied interest payment to the holder of the coupon every year as it approaches maturity."

"Ah yes, the bloody tax department: it's always there to complicate life and add costs to every transaction. You are right, Stewart. Because I bought the coupons at a discount, there is an implied annual receipt of interest, and someone is going to have to pay tax on that. In this case, the coupons would be pledged to you, but still be in my name for tax purposes."

"Wouldn't it be simpler if you just bought the coupons in bearer form and delivered them to me?" I asked.

"That's not possible, in that the coupons are never really delivered to you in paper form. They are kept by a broker as a book entry, with a purchaser's name assigned to them for tax purposes. This, of course, increases the cost of doing business in the coupon market, as it does for strip principals, which are also handled in a book-entry format. It would make life so much simpler if the taxation cowboys took their piece of the deal at the end of the life of the strip or coupon, but then someone would have had a tax deferral, which to them is worse than a case of athlete's foot. The simplest way of using strips is in a tax-free account, such as a pension scheme or in an offshore account."

I was starting to feel a chill and noticed that the sun was setting. I told Angelo I had overdosed on information and went up for a shower, seeing as we had a dinner date with the French couple.

9

*Is That Call
for Me?*

We arrived at the trattoria to find our acquaintances sipping Campari. It seemed like a good idea to me. The menu was fascinating — a main course of carpaccio with artichokes tempted me. For an appetizer, I chose an anchovy and tomato salad. This consisted of a slice of white onion, covered with a layer of thinly sliced beefsteak tomato, and topped with anchovies from Sciacca. These anchovies are considered the world's best and have a mild taste, yet beefy texture. The French Canadians kept pressing me for information about the bond market; I tried to think of how to best explain to them all the graphs Angelo had etched on the keel of his yacht.

"As I perceive it," I said, "if you understand the concept that yield is based on a fixed coupon or interest payment and changing price, the higher the interest payment on a bond, the less its price fluctuates during periods of changing interest rates. As well, the longer the maturity of a bond, the more its price will vary in a changing interest-rate environment, because the benefit or penalty for what you are holding increases the longer you must hold the paper to maturity."

Angelo slumped in his chair. "Is that all that is left of all those graphs I had to draw this morning? Are you reducing my efforts to a hundred words or less? You have ruined the Chinese proverb that 'one picture is worth a thousand words,'" Angelo moaned. "I expected less of you."

Gaston said, "That sounds reasonable to me. If I were to buy a high-coupon bond that always paid the same amount of interest, and interest rates fell, I would still own a large, ongoing stream of payments. These would be worth more than what the current, lower stream of payments would fetch. The longer the payments are guaranteed, the higher the price I can demand for my contract."

"That's a great term," I said. "You can look at a bond as a contract to pay out a fixed amount every year for a predetermined period."

"Okay, smart guys, how long is the period?" Angelo asked slyly.

"Obviously, to maturity," I said.

"What about the call feature?" Ang retorted.

"I am not completely conversant with that term," Gaston said.

"Although bonds may be issued for 20 years," Ang replied, "many of them have a call feature that allows the borrower to terminate the loan by repaying it before maturity. That privilege is accompanied by a premium redemption price, which declines over time. Typically, a 20-year bond would be callable for redemption after ten years at $1,010, with that premium declining by a tenth each year. Borrowers demand that call feature as insurance against their having made a bad prophecy about the future direction of interest rates. If you are the treasurer of a company that has issued an 8-percent coupon bond and interest rates fall to 6 percent, you would love to be able to redeem the existing bonds and refinance at the new, lower rate."

"I don't like that at all," I said. "Do I have the right to put the bond to the company?"

"If by that you mean being able to force the company to redeem your paper, then no. The treasurer does not want to come to work some morning with bondholders demanding their money back after it has already been invested. The only time that happens is when an issuer breaks some of the covenants of the bond indenture (contract), which requires the maintenance of certain working capital, an asset base, or other financial restrictions."

"That must throw all the yield calculations into a cocked hat," I snorted.

"It's not as disastrous as that. The bond traders quote yields to the first call date."

"Is there any way of guarding against the call feature?" Gaston asked.

"Yes. There are lots of bonds still in existence and trading that are now, and have been, callable for some time. In some cases, the interest rate on the bond is lower than what a new issue would demand. If the company called the bond, it would be faced with a higher net interest payment for a new issue than for the current one. You can be relatively certain that if a bond is trading at a discount from par and is callable, there is little likelihood of its being called. On the other hand, you may want to be wary of a high-coupon bond with a long maturity that seems cheap. The lower price indicates that it is now callable or very soon will be. The next question is, can the company find the funding to replace the current issue? Let me illustrate the point with the classic case of the Cleveland Electric Illuminating Company, or CEI, as it was known. In 1986, I bought an 8.75-percent bond issued by the company. Rates were high, and I got the paper at a discount from par. What particularly interested me in the bond was that it was due for redemption in 2003, but was callable in 1993. At the time I bought the bond, the State of Ohio had just deregulated the supply of power to the city of Cleveland. However, the asset backing the bonds was not the power-generating equipment but the distribution system. When interest rates fell in the 1990s, the company would have loved to refinance its debt by calling the high-coupon bonds and replacing them with new, lower-rate paper. Because of the uncertainty over the future of electricity generation in Cleveland, no potential buyers could be found for a bond issue backed by a power-distribution system in that city. So the bonds stayed in circulation until the company was bought by a nationwide utility that was absorbing all the local power-distribution systems. With their better credit rating and substantial financial resources, they were able to exercise the call feature and redeem the bonds in the low-interest scenario of the late 1990s."

"The call feature sounds like a nasty trick," I said.

"It is," Ang continued. "I don't understand how buyers of new issues can accept calls, but they do add a sense of adventure to what is a pedestrian market. If you see a bond with a call feature and can figure out what circumstances have deterred it from being exercised, there is a chance to make some money. The reasons are many. You have to know what was set out in the original indenture. Some bonds are only callable for a very precise period of time. Others are restricted by working capital or asset covenants. But one thing you know for sure is that if a bond was issued with a high interest rate, it is probably callable at some point in time before maturity. That said, if the company can't raise the money, the bond won't be called. I remember there was a Trump Casino bond outstanding for a long time that had a double-digit coupon in the order of about 11.25 percent, but was selling at a discount to yield 14 percent. At the time, rates were about 8 percent. But Donald Trump could not find anyone willing to refinance his existing bonds for less than 11.25 percent, so although callable, the bonds remained in circulation."

"Angelo, in the case of the Trump bonds, why didn't the Trump company buy back its own bonds?"

"Spoken like a true accountant. Of course, there is a benefit to the company in buying back its outstanding debt at a discount in the market and retire it. Most exchanges have rules that if the bond is not convertible, then the company has the right to buy back 10 percent of the issue annually. For convertibles, the rate is usually 5 percent, because securities regulators regard them as more akin to equity. Then again, if the debt is at a discount, what about the company's equity — its shares? If the shares are selling at less than the company's net asset value per share, or the book value, then a clever treasurer can buy back the company's shares and improve both corporate earnings and balance sheet measurements. There's the rub. If the company is out of favour with investors, then the treasurer can choose to buy back either equity or debt. If it is only the company's debt that is looked on with disdain, the treasurer will buy the debt back if the company can bankroll the move or can borrow in the short term to retire part of it. This will often show up as price support for junk bonds."

Gaston asked, "Do junk bonds always remain in that category?"

"Not always," Ang replied. "You see, if a company has fallen on hard times, then it could become a takeover candidate. In that case, the company that becomes the controlling interest is now responsible for the bonds, and the credit-rating agencies look at the credit worthiness of the acquirer. This offers a wonderful profit opportunity, since the good credit of the controlling company could eliminate the discount for risk, resulting in an overnight price hike for the bonds. It doesn't even have to be a reassessment of credit worthiness by the credit-rating agencies. Often the market will make that reappraisal. When the Government of Quebec's pension plan took a 53-percent ownership position in the real-estate company Cambridge Shopping Centres, the junk bonds jumped in price once the market realized that the bonds were now guaranteed by the Government of Quebec. Investors knew that the Quebec government would not be willing to lose its equity stake in Cambridge from a bond default. If the bond interest came due and the company was unable to pay, the pension plan would step in."

I remembered the real-estate debacle of the early 1990s. You could hardly give away a developer's bonds. But, at the same time, the bonds of a major office-building developer were selling at a premium. I asked Ang if he remembered those.

"Yeah. In that case, the 11.25-percent bonds were a first

mortgage bond on a premium downtown tower. The second mortgage on the tower was held by a bank. The bank was not about to see the building fall into the hands of the first mort- gagers, and so it paid the interest on those bonds out of its own pocket to prevent a default."

"It would seem," Gaston said, "that this junk-bond arena is not for the amateur."

"That is an interesting statement," I replied. "Amateur investors will often buy shares of companies they know little about, without much trepidation."

Ang said, "There is a difference. In most cases, part-time investors are really speculators. They are buying a share with the intention of selling it soon after. Junk-bond buyers are actually investing to get a return. They want to know that the stream of income they are purchasing will continue, and that they will get their principal back at the end of the day.

"It used to be that the buyer of junk bonds had to do a lot of financial analysis. As the market has expanded, this chore has been taken over by the financial analysts at some of the brokerage houses. They publish monthly tomes showing the financial strength of these companies. The most critical number to the junk-bond buyer is the cash flow, often shown as EBITDA — translated into English, this stands for 'Earnings Before Interest, Taxes, Depreciation, and Amortization.' If you want to know if a company can pay its interest, you obviously don't want to double count that figure, so you add it back to the reported earnings. Taxes are payable after interest expense; therefore that has to be added back, too. Both depreciation and amortization are non-cash charges, and therefore diminish the reported earnings without affecting the cash available to pay interest. Obviously, you want this number to be as high as possible and at least equal to the annual total interest cost of the company. The brokerage analysts will show in their reports the number of times the EBITDA covers the interest. A company could report a loss on its income statement and still show an interest coverage of two or three times. The EBITDA number tells you the strength of the company's ability to pay its interest.

"Another interesting number is the debt-to-equity ratio. There are two measures here. If a company has $75 million in equity and $25 million in debt, then its debt-to-equity ratio is three to one. This tells you that there is market-perceived value of the company's equity of $3 for every $1 of debt. You can then conclude that there is a considerable amount of shareholder investment to run through before affecting the debt-holders."

"Angelo, you mentioned there were two measures in the debt-to-equity measurement," I said.

"Oh yes, I almost forgot. You see, there is the market value of equity, and then there is the book value. The market value is simply the total quoted value of all the common and preferred shares. The book value is obtained from the balance sheet, and is calculated by adding together the retained earnings and shareholder equity shown in the financial statements."

Gaston asked, "Shouldn't those be the same?"

"Unlikely," Angelo replied. "The book value from the balance sheet is historical, while the market price is active. Think of an oil company that has spent $20 million developing an oil field that is worth $10 billion at $25-per-barrel oil prices. On the balance sheet, that asset would be valued at $20 million while in the marketplace the share price would reflect the $10 billion. As a result, the calculated value of the firm, or book value, is usually less than the market value. Obviously, if the oil price falls, the value of the asset falls; in turn, the share price will fall, changing the market value of the firm. The book value would remain unchanged."

"Which value is the best one to use, market or book?" I asked.

"The market value gives you the best answer in most cases. There are always exceptions, though. The market value is determined by what investors perceive the price of the shares should be. Like any perception, that can be false. Once you understand that 65 percent of the movement of a share price owes to the action of the market, you can see that the price of the equity can swing with the ups and downs of investor sentiment — not a particularly useful indicator when trying to determine what equity the company has backing the debt. This was most clearly exemplified by the Oxford Development situation. During the low point of the market cycle in the 1990s, the Oxford debentures traded down to ten cents on the dollar. This low price was occasioned by investors attaching a very low value to the company's real estate, which consisted of some very valuable office buildings. When the company was refinanced, the bondholders were paid off in shares, which eventually were equivalent to par for the old bonds."

"Mon dieu!" Gaston uttered. "That is a ten-for-one gain — an incredible investment performance."

"In whose eyes?" Angelo replied. "The junk bondholders had to give up the stream of interest payments they thought they had purchased. Although they were well rewarded for their patience, I can remember having to hold some sweaty hands while the situation worked itself out. Few of the bond-holders stayed the course to the full appreciation of the shares they were given in exchange for their debentures. Some were content just to get their investment back, and happy with the high yield they received while the company was in difficulty."

"This sounds rather scary," I said.

"Shares go up and down and you don't think that's scary," Angelo replied. "When you buy equity in a company, you probably know less about the finances of the company than most junk-bond buyers. When Oxford was refinanced, the shareholders got crumbs while the bondholders got the whole cake. When companies such as Oxford get themselves into trouble, they immediately interest the vulture funds, who most often buy the debt and eschew the shares of the fallen angel. There is almost always some residual value in the bonds, and these can usually be bought at a significant discount from their intrinsic value. Why? The fund manager holding the Oxfords in his portfolio does not want to endure the uncertainty of waiting for the company's problems to resolve. He prefers instead the certainty of a bid from the vultures for his position in the bonds."

"I don't know if I have the stomach for the junk market," I said.

"Remember that, of the lowest-rated bonds, only 3 percent defaulted in the last 20 years, while during the 40 years from 1924 to 1964 only 4 percent failed."

"Have you ever owned an Internet stock?" Gaston asked.

"Of course I have," I replied.

"If you can stand the level of risk in buying shares in companies with no foreseeable prospect for earnings, yet are worried about the possibility of not getting your interest from a functioning company, you should reassess your values."

Gaston had a good point. I remembered seeing a list in the financial pages of convertible bonds in operating companies with yields of 9 percent and higher. I had grown up in the era of equity, and the idea of investing rather than speculating was foreign to me. But it was obvious that Angelo had found a kindred spirit in Gaston.

I had a tiramisu for dessert. The trattoria's version consisted of a layer of Amaretto cookies soaked in yet more Amaretto, then covered by a layer of whipped cream and some other artery cloggers I couldn't identify. I realized I didn't need to worry about my retirement savings. If I kept eating with Angelo, I would die a fat, happy, youngish man.

10

Dirty Words

Before I could finish dessert, Michelle exclaimed, "But what about inflation?"

I felt as though a hush had fallen over the trattoria, and every pair of eyes was suddenly focused on us. Would we be asked to leave?

"That is a terrible word, but you are right, Michelle, we will have to address that threat," Ang replied. "First, you have to recognize that inflation is a government-induced phenomenon. Its first manifestation was recorded by Aristophanes in his play *The Wasps*:

> *Where is that silver drachma of old,*
> *And the recent gold coins,*
> *So clear stamped and worth their weight*
> *Through the known world,*
> *Have ceased to circulate.*

Now Athenian shoppers go to market,
With their pockets full of shoddy silver-plated coppers.

The Athenian government, in its efforts to pay for the Peloponnesian War, began to debase the silver coinage of the period by adding base metals to it, until finally the entire coin was copper and covered with a silver plating.

"The next recorded use of inflation was by Louis XIV of France. He was having trouble paying for his new palace at Versailles, so he doubled the amount of paper currency in circulation. That, of course, caused an economic collapse, which contributed to the French Revolution. You currently see economies being ruined all over Africa through the use of the printing press as a financial instrument."

"But, Angelo, surely governments must by now know the terrible effects of inflation. Why do they keep doing it?" I asked.

"This reminds me of the story of the scorpion and the frog. A scorpion was standing on the edge of the river as a frog paddled by. The scorpion asked the frog to take him across the river on his back. The frog replied that if he did that, the scorpion would sting him and the frog would die. The scorpion replied that it would be absurd for him to sting the frog in mid-stream, as they would both die. The frog accepted this logic and began to paddle across the stream with the scorpion on his back. In mid-stream, the frog felt a searing pain in his back from the scorpion's sting. When the frog asked why he did it, surely knowing that they would both be doomed, the scorpion replied, 'I had to, It's my nature.' So it is with governments. They know that inflation is a deadly financial poison, but they always resort to it."

"But why?" Gaston asked.

"General coffers," I replied. "I've seen it time and again. Governments have moved away from specific taxes, instead lumping them all together. In that way, you can't tell if the road tax collected at the gas pump is being used for the roads or to bribe some voter. Take, for instance, the health care system in Canada. Recent numbers have shown expenditures of about $2,200 per person, while the amount collected is $11,000, yet the health care system is still underfunded. So what happened to the taxpayer money we all thought was being collected for hospitals and doctors? It likely paid for a former prime minister's love nest and jet planes to fly insignificant ministers around. The one taxation pool that was earmarked, the pension system, has been bankrupted, and the populace is howling at the obvious foul-up. No more open books on that one. So the government must always increase taxation, because it has no checks and balances. The most all-encompassing form of taxation is inflation."

"Stewart is correct," Ang said. "It is the most efficient and effective form of taxation. Everyone but the government sees a decline in wealth. Stock and bond markets collapse, and unemployment increases, as does poverty. What the government experiences is an increase in tax revenues, and a decrease in its debts and liabilities. The thousand dollars of purchasing power borrowed ten years ago by the government is paid back, post-inflation, with less purchasing power, although still nominally a thousand dollars. A pension payment of $600 per month after a good bout of inflation will only purchase a week's groceries. That is why the pension plans of government members are always indexed to inflation, while those of taxpayers are unindexed."

"That's as horrible as I remember it being in the 1970s,"

I said. "But how do I protect myself? Shouldn't I be in equities?"

"No. Equities suffer as well, because of the depreciation in the tax filings. Corporate earnings, and hence taxes, are adjusted for capital investments through depreciation. As a result of inflation, the amount being charged for depreciation won't allow the corporation to have enough after-tax income to replace its deteriorating assets. Only those companies with hard assets, such as real estate or natural resources, see some stability in their share prices. The rest collapse."

"Can you explain that?" Gaston asked.

Angelo grabbed a napkin and produced the following figures:

Pre-inflation cost of equipment	$1,000,000
Post-inflation cost of equipment	$3,000,000
Pre-inflation tax statement	
Earnings	$2,000,000
Write-off of equipment	$1,000,000
Taxable income	$1,000,000
Tax @ 25%	$250,000
Funds left with the corporation	$1,750,000

"As you can see," Ang said, "the corporation has a profit and funds left to replace its equipment because of the write-off. Now, if inflation is induced, the profit will increase dramatically, because the corporation is earning more, smaller dollars. Assume 100-percent inflation and the scenario looks like this:

Earnings	$4,000,000
Write-off of equipment	$1,000,000
Taxable income	$3,000,000
Tax	$750,000
Funds left with the corporation	$2,250,000

"At first glance, it looks like the corporation is better off by $500,000. However, in reality, the company cannot continue to operate, because inflation has boosted the cost of its replacement equipment to $3,000,000, and it cannot afford to replace its equipment. The taxing authority has trebled its take. This explains why stock markets fall in times of inflation: the effective rate of taxation is increased, forcing companies to borrow to replace their aging plants, rather than using internally generated funds for that purpose.

"There are, however, safety hatches for the bond investor. The first of these is the foreign bond. Let me sketch out for you what the value of the Canadian dollar has been in Swiss francs and U.S. dollars on an indexed basis."

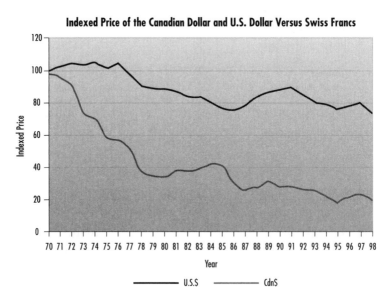

Indexed Price of the Canadian Dollar and U.S. Dollar Versus Swiss Francs

"What the chart shows you is that, to buy a Canadian dollar today, it would cost the Swiss a quarter of what they had to pay for that same dollar 30 years ago. To purchase American currency, the Swiss need only cough up three-quarters of the cash needed back then. You can say either foreign currencies have become more expensive, or the Canadian buck a lot cheaper.

"Obviously, if your older bond holdings are in Swiss francs, they are now worth more in U.S. or Canadian dollars than what you paid for them. For example, if you bought 40,000 Swiss francs of 4.5-percent coupon, 30-year bonds, worth roughly $10,000 Canadian in 1970, they would still be worth 40,000 Swiss francs today, but would be equal to $40,000 Canadian at maturity. Further, you would have been paid an average of $27,000 Canadian in interest. There are many countries like Switzerland where inflation is a dirty word. Germany is another one. These countries are loath to allow rampant inflation to take hold in their economies.

In the U.S., where innovation is the nation's forte, the government has come up with an inflation-protected bond. In 1997, the U.S. Treasury issued an instrument called the Treasury Inflation Protection Securities, or TIPS for short. The principal amount of the bond was indexed to inflation, although the coupon amount stayed constant. Therefore, in the case of the original 3.375-percent bond, the $1,000 par value was raised incrementally by the Treasury on a monthly basis for the amount of inflation indicated by the Consumer Price Index. When the bond matures in 2007, the principal amount of the bond could be as high as $1,200. In other words, for every $1,000 par value you purchased, you could receive $1,200. However, there are disadvantages.

"The added value attached to the bond is considered income by the Internal Revenue Service and taxed in the year applied. Note that I said applied; the recipient of the added value does not obtain it until the bond is sold or redeemed. These bonds, when held in a tax-deferred account, such as an IRA, a 401k, or an RRSP, make great sense, since the tax is not applicable and the holder gets the benefit of inflation protection."

"That seems complicated to me," I said.

Angelo retorted, "I didn't say that America was the home of simplicity, only ingenuity. Other countries have tackled inflation protection in a much simpler way by adjusting the rate of interest paid to reflect inflation. There are a number of floating-rate, long-term bonds where the interest rate is adjusted annually to reflect the change in some benchmark lending rate, such as the London Interbank Borrowing Rate, or LIBOR. Typically, a bond will pay LIBOR plus a given premium. The LIBOR rate, or any national bank's prime lending rate, will include the trend of inflation, thus insuring the investor receives a return that encompasses the loss of purchasing power."

"That's not complete protection," Gaston interjected, "because you still lose the value of the capital you invested. The $1,000 of purchasing power you lent out is returned with diminished strength. Is there not something better?"

"Another shield from inflation is the hard asset–backed bond," Angelo replied. "There are bonds that can be exchanged for fixed amounts of gold. These are often issued with a skimpy interest rate, because they are inflation-protected. Remember the old U.S. five-dollar bills? Many of them were silver certificates exchangeable at the U.S. mint for four ounces of silver. They are gone now, as are most other asset-backed currencies, but there are still bonds out there backed by gold or gold shares. The price of gold and gold-company shares rises with inflation.

"The demonetizing of gold by major nations indicates one of two things: either governments believe that inflation is impossible under current financial market structures, or they don't want to be fettered if they wish to impose inflation. The current use of derivatives and other financial instruments makes inducing inflation difficult, because bond yields increase instantaneously at the first whiff of inflation. It's now more difficult for governments to get away with inflation, but like the frog you have to remember the nature of the beast."

"But why not flee to the stock markets of countries with low or no inflation when the domestic scene is victimized?"

"That is a consideration, Stewart, but which stocks would you buy in, say, the Swiss market? You know little about the growth of the various sectors of the Swiss market, and even less about the companies within those markets. For the bond investor, life is much simpler. To begin with, bond investors can buy governments. There are Canadian and Australian government bonds — not to mention those of other countries — at different governmental levels, in all the major currencies. If a bond investor wants to move down the quality curve, he can find local and foreign corporate bonds in the various currencies, like an Air Canada issue in Swiss francs or a Ford Motor bond in British pounds. To make life even simpler, the rating agencies make no distinction between currencies when assessing the bonds of a corporation."

This was great. I could buy bonds issued by companies and governments I was familiar with in any currency I wanted. The Air Canada bond in Swiss francs that Angelo had mentioned would even be RRSP-eligible, and I could bet there were others like it.

It was a quiet walk home for me to my little villa. As I thought about what I had learned, it began to make sense. My concern now was: had I learned enough?

11

~~⌣~~

Quality vs.Discrimination: The Liberals' Dilemma

I went to my usual coffee shop in Viareggio, where the locals now greeted me with *buono giorno* while offering me a shot of grappa. I tried it once, only to discover that it really was firewater, and best suited to preventing car radiators from freezing. As usual, there was an ongoing debate. Yesterday's concerned the doping of athletes, while today's concerned the question of which prime minister had stolen the most from the treasury. The discussion broke down when one chap insisted that inflation should be factored in, while another said that it was unfair to dwell only on the prime minister when the whole cabinet was on the take. My Italian isn't that good, so I had to make do with Aldo Moro, Berlisconi, Black Friar's Bridge, Banco di Roma, and a few other well-known terms, but it was fun. When gales of laughter broke out, I asked the bartender what the joke was. He explained that a famous pornographic movie star had been elected to government, and one of the wags had suggested that only porn stars be allowed to run for government — since they performed naked, they didn't have pockets to stuff with ill-gotten money. As I wandered off to the boatyard, I thought about how often humour approached the truth.

Upon arrival, I found that Angelo had used a rotating sander to lightly buff the hull of the boat. We had finished with the paint removal the previous day, and were now preparing to apply the barrier coat to the hull. We applied masking tape to the waterline, and Angelo began mixing a can of green paint. I asked him about it.

"Not paint, Stew, epoxy. It is a two-component material that will harden in about 30 minutes, so we have to work quickly."

"That's not much time to apply a gallon," I said. "Isn't there something better with a slower drying time?"

"This is the best there is. Life is full of compromises. Which reminds me: we ended yesterday with the questions of quality in the bond market."

"Yeah. As I remember, you said that the rating agencies determined the quality of bonds. Are they reliable?"

"First, Stew, you have to define quality. In the bond market, quality is determined by the ability to pay not only the ongoing stream of interest but also the principal at maturity. The quality rating applied to a bond represents the likelihood of those two events occurring. The higher the rating, the better your chances; like any investment, though, there is never certainty. There have been bonds issued with a high rating that eventually went into default. Remember that the people doing the rating are human, too, with all the biases of today and no special prescience allowing them to see into the future. If a company can't pay either its interest or its principal when due, then it is forced into bankruptcy."

We were applying Angelo's green liquid at a ferocious rate, but I noticed that it was drying almost as quickly as it we could put it on the hull. It turned out to be amazing stuff. I had touched my work pants with fingers covered in the epoxy only to find that the marks outlasted the pants. If only investments could be made of epoxy!

"I understand, Ang, that in bankruptcy, the assets are dispersed in the following sequence: tax department, bank loans, trade accounts, bondholders, and, finally, shareholders. Usually the last two in the sequence are the worst hit."

"Yes," Ang replied, "it is odd that when shareholders buy the stock, they never ask whether the company will survive. With bond buyers, it is always the first question. If a default occurs, the shareholders seldom get a dime. The bondholders might if there are real assets in the company."

"Define real assets."

"Well, let's say there are two companies on the verge of bankruptcy. One has an inventory of high-fashion dresses as its assets while the other has timberlands. Obviously, you are more likely to get some remnant value out of the trees than the dresses. The trees are a real hard asset with a prescribed value. But assume, then, that the trees are in Indonesia. They may be of high-value teak, but the investors' ability to realize that value could be encumbered by politics or graft.

"In answer to your question, real assets are those things that have an ongoing value you can realize. All natural resources and real estate fall into that category. A modern production facility with demand for the output could also be classified as a real asset. But the assets also have to be in a jurisdiction where the rule of law applies. The hierarchy for asset security, by country, is the U.S., Canada, and the European Union. Outside those jurisdictions, it is difficult for creditors to obtain title, through seizure, to the assets pledged against the indebtedness. Lenders to Asia made a similar rude discovery during the recent financial troubles there. Although assets had been pledged against the loans, it was impossible to force companies into bankruptcy to obtain the assets needed to offset the loan principal. I think it is sufficient to say that the farther away your investments are from North America, the greater your risk."

"It would seem to me," I said, "that the only really secure loan is a government loan."

"If you believe that, then look at the walls of many of today's brokerage houses, which are festooned with bond certificates from the Chinese and Russian governments. One of the absurd beliefs in the bond market is that government bonds are more secure than corporates, because governments have the ability to tax, and therefore have an infinite source of funds. That's exactly what recent investors in Russian and Mexican government bonds believed, only to find that it was not true. Even Canada has had its foreign debt downgraded as a result of its deteriorating ability to tax. The Laffer curve eventually catches up with you, and the higher you raise taxes, the less you collect."

"What is the Laffer curve, Ang?"

At this point, Angelo took one of the smaller brushes and sketched the following graph on the concrete floor of the boatyard. He explained that the U.S. government had a 7-percent tax rate in the early 1900s but, some 20 years later, collected the same revenue with a 77-percent tax rate.

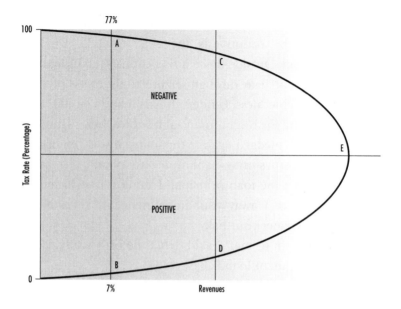

"As you can see, when tax rates pass 50 percent," Angelo continued, "the amount of revenue generated starts to decrease as people begin to avoid and evade taxes."

"You've painted the boatyard floor with epoxy, which will probably be here for eternity," I said.

"Yeah, and it will probably take until eternity for those government goofs to figure out the effects of excessive taxation. Maybe the archaeologists will look at this in the centuries to come and understand what lead to the demise of Western civilization."

"So, if I understand you correctly," I said, "there comes a point of diminishing returns from taxation."

"Correct. A spendthrift or corrupt government will find itself in the position of having tax revenue fall short of the interest requirements. The usual governmental solution to this is to try to inflate the currency, which then leads to lenders demanding higher interest rates to compensate for the inflation. In this scenario, you see the hard-currency bonds of the government go to a higher yield, and the government's local-currency bonds would trade to yield even higher double-digit rates, reflecting the fear of default."

"What happens if a government defaults?" I asked.

"You end up with a fancy engraving to hang on your wall."

"But I see that the Mexican government is once again issuing bonds."

"The new issues are backed not only by the government's pledge to pay, but also by oil reserves. This gives investors at least some confidence they will see their capital returned should the Mexican government once again default on interest payments. At the same time, though, the bonds are selling at 400 basis points* over U.S. government issues, indicating that there is still some trepidation in the minds of investors as to the quality. You have to remember, Stew, that the barrels of oil being pledged against the Mexican loans were, in effect, stolen from other investors prior to World War II through nationalization. Who is to say that the oil won't be stolen again? When purchasing government bonds, don't delude yourself by investing in the paper of some tinpot despot, sham democracy, or lawless regime. When government paper is being offered to you at a yield substantially higher than that of the U.S., you have to ask yourself why."

"Then, as I understand it, Ang, the hierarchy of bond quality would be as follows:

---

* One hundred basis points is equivalent to 1 percent. Therefore, 400 basis points is 4 percent.

- Government bonds issued by strong countries
- Bank debentures
- Utility-company debentures
- Blue chip–company debentures
- First mortgage bonds
- The rest of the bond universe

"Stewart, I've always admired you as a fast learner. But remember that quality, like beauty, is in the eye of the beholder."

12

Looking over the Rhododendron

I was satisfied with what I had learned. I could see some interesting potential for the funds kept offshore for my future benefit. I had an uncle who resided in Ireland but kept his wealth in tax havens. He had arranged that his inheritors, upon his death, could set up their particular pieces of his estate in the most tax-efficient manner possible. In my case, the estate would set up a trust in a tax haven to hold my inheritance.* In this way, the inheritance wouldn't be stuck in North America, where it could be seized by some suit-happy lawyer, and the assets could grow tax free until I retired. I hoped to retire to some tax-friendly regime and take my inheritance at that time.

The interesting feature of the inheritance was that it could earn interest tax free. If I wanted to net 6 percent per year in

---

* See my book, *My Blue Haven.*

the trust, that was all I had to receive. My counterparts in the taxable regime would have to earn 12 percent in interest, or 10 percent in capital gains, to match my return. They, of course, would have to triple their risk profiles to do so.

I shared my thoughts with Angelo. "A bond investment makes great sense for an offshore account. According to the figures you gave me early on, medium-quality corporate bonds yield 5.75 percent after inflation, while stocks offer 6 percent. I could load up my offshore fund or self-administered pension plan with reasonable debentures and have a fine nest egg at retirement."

"Actually, Stewart, it gets better than that. You could use what we call a hedge in the bond universe — and please, no puns. It involves selling one security short and offsetting it with the purchase of another. Although not a legal manoeuvre for your self-directed pension plan, it can be a great benefit to the offshore account.

"Imagine a corporation issues 8-percent debentures, which are convertible at the holder's discretion into shares at a rate of 50 shares per debenture. The debenture is said to have a $20 conversion price, since the $1,000 paid for that debenture can be converted into 50 shares, at the cost of $20 per share ($20 x 50 shares = $1000). Assume that in the current market environment, the shares have fallen and are selling at $16 each. A clever investor decides to buy $100,000 of the debentures at par. At the same time, he sells short 5,000 shares (one $1,000 debenture converts into 50 shares, giving our investor the right to acquire 100 x 50 shares = 5,000) at $16. Let's now look at his brokerage statement." Ang sketched the following:

Debit	$100,000	paid out for the purchase of 100 debentures at $1,000
Credit	$80,000	received from the sale of 5,000 shares at $16
Cash	$20,000	investment required from client

"The result of this operation is that the client is holding $100,000 of 8-percent-coupon bonds with a $20,000 investment! In broker parlance, this $20,000 is called the spread of the hedge. The impact of the investor's low cost is dramatic, as shown on his income statement. Have a look." Angelo continued his scribbles with the following:

Debenture income	$100,000 x 8% = $8,000
Cost of borrowing shares	$80,000 x 1% stock borrowing fee = ($800)
Annual cash flow	$7,200
Annual return on investment	$7,200 ÷ $20,000 = 36%

"The return could be diminished by the margin requirements of the broker, but the final return should be better than 25 percent."

"Angelo," I said, "that is awesome. I can't believe that a person can make 36 percent on his money without considerable risk."

"No investment is riskless, but for this one, the risk is very low. In this particular example, for instance, there are still some financing wrinkles. The investor's yield is slightly less than the 36 percent I showed you for simplicity, because the $800 is paid in monthly instalments. As such, it costs him slightly more than the annual $800 payment shown. There is also the question of dividends. If the shares paid a dividend, the short seller would have to pay that amount to the purchaser of the 5,000 shares sold short. However, companies that have to issue debentures with a convertible feature are seldom in the position to pay dividends."

"Let's look, then, at the risks of this particular investment. For one thing, the share price could go up. If it does, the value of the convertible debenture would rise. If the price of the shares rises to $25 each, then the value of the debenture would increase to something approximating $1,250. At par, the debentures convert with a $20 share price (50 shares per debenture); the additional $5 per share adds $250 (50 shares per debenture x $5) to each debenture's value, for a total in this case of $25,000 (100 bonds x $250). But the cost of the short sell would rise as well, requiring the investor to post a further $45,000 of collateral (the difference between the $16 and $25 share price, or $9 x 5,000 shares). However, after deducting the increase in the value of the debentures, there is only a shortfall of $20,000 ($45,000 share price increase – $25,000 debenture price increase). The investor would see a margin call from his broker for $10,000, because this is an equity debit requiring a 50-percent margin. On the brokerage statement it would look like this." Angelo showed me the calculations as follows:

Debit	($100,000)	from the purchase of debentures
Credit	$80,000	from the sale of shares
Cash	$20,000	original investment to meet 20% margin
	$45,000	increased share value
	$25,000	increased debenture value
Balance	$20,000	shortfall in account
Required	$10,000	further investment

As Angelo continued to show me, the brokerage income account would look like this:

Net income	$7,200
Yield	$7,200 ÷ $30,000 = 24%

"At this point, with his yield having fallen to 24 percent from 36 percent, the investor might want to consider unwinding the position. This is risky, though, because the bond price may not track the rising share price perfectly. Instead of selling his debenture at the equivalent share price, he might get slightly less if he tries to unwind the hedge. It is unlikely, however, that the markets would be so inefficient as to cost him as much as his annual interest benefit.

"On the other hand, the price of the shares could fall, which would lead to a profit. Assume that the price of the shares falls to $14. Then the current value of the shares would be $70,000 (5,000 x $14). The account has $10,000 unrealized gain, since it sold the shares for $80,000 with a potential purchase price of $70,000. The investor could now unwind his position with a gain, or reduce the cash component to increase his yield. As for the debenture, its price would be supported by the yield."

"Angelo, these hedges must be dynamite in an untaxed account, but what happens if the bonds are called?"

"Most corporate treasurers would rather issue shares than debt, because, in their eyes, the shares have no associated cost, while the debentures require the payment of interest. Therefore, they seldom call the debentures unless the paper is trading at a premium. Investors, seeing their debentures trading at a premium because the underlying shares at conversion are worth more than par, will choose to convert rather than redeem the debentures. The corporation's treasurer then acquires new shareholders, and is thereby no longer responsible for paying out cash for either debenture redemption or interest to those holders."

"Well, what if the company goes bankrupt?" I asked.

"The hedge holder will see the shares go to a minimal value or be worthless. Therefore, the short sale has a replacement cost of zero. In the example I showed you, the hedge player received $80,000 for selling the shares short. If the company is bankrupt, his purchase price might be $10 to cover his entire position. As a bondholder, he might be able to obtain some salvage value as a result of the sale of the corporate assets. The hedge investor would, in the above example, need only obtain 20 cents on the dollar to break even. There haven't been many bankruptcies in recent years where the creditors received less than 20 cents on the dollar."

"If these hedges are so spectacular, why don't we see more people using them?"

"Stewart, you have to have two sides of a deal. You don't want to pay an absurd premium for the debentures, as this would just drive down your yield. On the other side of the deal is the short sale. There is a well-known adage in the investment business that says, 'Never chase a short.' This means that an investor is foolish to try to short a stock while the price is declining. If the value at which the short is undertaken is excessively low, the share price could rise, destroying the benefits of the hedge. Many corporate treasurers are surprised to see a dramatic share price decline at the time of a convertible-debenture issue; this effect is caused by hedge players' positioning themselves by short selling the stock against the convertible. When the difference between the exercise price of the bond conversion and the market price reaches what the traders consider rational, further hedge positions become uneconomic.

"You have to be aware, as well, that some of the hedge positions may be undertaken by professional short sellers.

The potential loss for a short seller is unlimited. He can protect himself by buying call options on the shares he has shorted, or by buying the company's convertible debentures, which are another form of call option."

"I'm going to look into some hedges for my offshore account," I said.

"Don't be so quick, Stewart. The short seller needs to constantly monitor the performance of the two securities involved. Hedging is therefore best left in the hands of professionals, as in a bond fund."

"I've been wanting to ask you about those."

13

The Fun of Funds

"I have a nickname for bond fund investors: the loafer crowd. They are too lazy to take the little time necessary to understand the bond market, and they wear loafer-type shoes, because they are too lazy to tie the laces of oxfords. The only people I can forgive are those who invest in hedges."

"The management fee charged by bond funds can be as high as 1.5 percent or as low as 0.5 percent. I have to ask what the investor is getting for this price. It doesn't take a rocket scientist to buy government bonds, and corporates, which do require some balance sheet analysis, usually make up a minor part of the portfolio.

"Then there is the problem of maturity. If you want to take out your funds in five years, why would you buy a fund with a ten-year duration? You would be better to invest on your own in a bunch of five-year bonds."

"Angelo, this sounds a little too pedantic for me. You know

there are fund buyers out there in investorland who just want to park their money for a brief stint while the equity market cools."

"I see," he replied. "You're talking about the folks who buy at the bottom and sell at the top. Do you know who those people are?"

"No."

"They are liars. If 75 percent of stock-market professionals underperform the market, and 80 percent of commodity speculators lose (except for that stellar trader, Hillary Clinton*), who are these people selling out of equities at the top to buy bonds?"

"Ang, I didn't say that they were selling at the top. I said they wanted to park their money."

"There you go again, assuming that the bond market is a temporary alternative to the stock market. The truth is that for full-grown adults anticipating retirement within the next ten years or already retired, the bond market is where the majority of their funds should be invested. Remember, if they lose a bundle in one of the market crashes, they don't have a lifetime to recoup the loss.

"If you are hell-bent on using a fund to invest in the bond market, then rest assured that there is the usual collection of good, bad, and ugly funds out there. There are funds that out-perform the bond indices in both yield and appreciation. However, these are not pure buy-and-hold funds, but are actively managed using more than just the hedging technique

---

* Hillary Clinton purchased a small position in an agricultural commodity early one day in the 1980s. During the interday trading she sold out her position and made $10,000. That would seem brilliant enough. However, even more ingenious was the fact that she discontinued trading. She therefore is the only person with a perfect record as a com-modity trader, as unlikely as that may seem."

we discussed to increase their performance. As with any investment, the essential part of the deal is investigating before buying.

"It is important that investors know to what extent the fund uses unconventional resources to enhance the fund yield. Then there is the question of taxation. In the case of your inheritance, Stewart, you want a fund that will pay you gross without the deduction of withholding or income taxes. Funds that use short-term loans as part of their portfolios would be subject to withholding tax on any profits generated by the short-term investments that were then exported off-shore. Withholding taxes have to be collected by the institution that disburses the funds to a non-resident, or be paid by the institution from its own pocket. Collecting from the investor after the fact is often difficult, as taxes are not a debt, and court enforcement on the part of any organization but the government is virtually impossible. So, for the offshore investor, unconventional bond funds prove problematic."

"Under those circumstances, how can I have the benefit of a bond fund offshore?' I asked.

"The simplest route is to ask for the most recent fund statements and look at what they are holding. Then mimic the portfolio, or cherry-pick for what you consider to be the best components."

"Okay, Ang, I'm sold. What are the mechanics?"

"Here is the bad news. The bond markets are seldom trans-parent. There are a few bonds listed on exchanges, but primarily they are traded on a market-maker basis. This means that someone sitting at a desk somewhere is offering to buy or sell a particular issue at some price spread. If it is a commonly traded government issue, the spread would be small between the price offered to sell and the one to buy. A U.S. Treasury 30-year bond of 5.75 percent would be offered, for instance, at $96.25 and bid at $96, meaning that if you wanted to buy from the dealer, it would cost you $962.50 for the bond. If you wanted to sell, the dealer would buy from you at $960. There is a spread, or difference, of $2.50 in the two prices. However, when you get into less heavily traded issues or those with lower credit ratings, the spreads increase to cover the dealer's risk. So a Trump Casino 11.25-percent could be offered at $115 and bid $112 — a $30 spread. The bonds are bought and sold at bond desks, and there is someone offering to buy or sell virtually every bond at some firm. The bond desks operate as entities separate from the share-trading operation at the brokerage house, and trade as principals, meaning that they buy from or sell to you and every other client. When you call your stockbroker and ask for a bond quote, the broker will hopefully be able to obtain a price from the bond desk and then tack on a fee to give you a final price. Seldom will you be able to obtain a spread price on an unlisted corporate bond."

"What do you mean by 'hopefully'?" I asked.

"Because the bond desks are a separate profit centre, they operate for themselves. Whereas the research, trading, and back-office sectors of a firm are acting to help the broker facilitate the client, the bond desk works only for the bond desk. I still manage a lot of retirement money for my friends, and when I want to make changes in portfolios I have to use large brokerage houses for big orders and small players for individual orders. When I wanted to buy 20,000 Swiss-franc par-value Air Canada debentures from a large dealer, I was told it only dealt in lots of 100,000. I had to bundle a bunch of orders to get to that threshold. Even then, I found that the bond prices differed by as much as 30 francs per bond at the various dealers. In other words, you have to shop for bonds. Often, when I'm told that I'm below the threshold at a large bank dealer, I can find another, smaller brokerage that will do the trade."

14

The Huckleberry Finn Approach

Angelo's hull was painted, Sarah's culinary skills were honed, and we were back on a 747 heading home. I was reading a copy of the *Financial Times* of London when Sarah asked, "What do you think of the stock market at this point?"

"Looks toppy. The Dow Jones is trading at 34 times earnings, while the long bond is at 6.75 percent. That translates into an earnings yield of 3 percent for shares, compared to 6 for bonds. It can't last."

"What are you going to do, Stewart? You can't just sit there and leave all our savings in shares."

"Not a problem, my dear. I am going to build us a nice bond portfolio."

"What do you know about the bond market?"

"Actually, quite a bit."

"Then tell me," she said.

I immediately thought of Angelo's trick: to exchange information for labour. "I will, my dear, but I was thinking that a more appropriate place and time would be in the basement at home."

"Why there?"

"I thought you could help me refinish that beautiful mahogany table we've had for some time. We could chat and work at the same time."

"Gosh, Stew, I'm not sure I'm that interested."

About the Author

Alex Doulis was born in Vancouver in 1939 and graduated from the University of British Columbia.

He worked for a number of years as a geologist in Alaska and the Yukon. He was also employed in Utah and Ontario as a mathematician in the early days of computers. His field of endeavour was the application of computers to the analysis of financial problems. He took this experience to the investment industry, where he toiled for 19 years.

While on Bay Street, he was one of the highest-ranked analysts in his field, a partner at Gordon Securities, and a director of McNeil Mantha.

He has spent the past ten years living tax free on his yacht in the Mediterranean and travelling.

You may contact the author at his website **www.alexdoulis.com** or at:

P.O. Box 378
Providenciales, Turks & Caicos Islands
British West Indies

Buy low ~~yield~~ coupon secondary
in high rate environment
- will buy at discount
- have the current rate yield
- and if rates fall the gain
  will be greatest